The Syntax of V-V Resultatives in Mandarin Chinese

Jianxun Liu

The Syntax of V-V Resultatives in Mandarin Chinese

 Springer

Jianxun Liu
Department of Linguistics
University of Victoria
Victoria, BC, Canada

ISBN 978-981-33-6845-3   ISBN 978-981-33-6846-0   (eBook)
https://doi.org/10.1007/978-981-33-6846-0

This Springer imprint is published by the registered company Springer Nature Singapore Pte Ltd.
The registered company address is: 152 Beach Road, #21-01/04 Gateway East, Singapore 189721,
Singapore

Acknowledgements

This book is my 2019 Ph.D. dissertation at the University of Victoria, Canada. Looking back over the years of writing this book, there are many people I want to thank.

First of all, I want to express my deepest gratitude to my supervisor of doctorial study, Dr. Martha McGinnis. Dr. McGinnis has largely changed my view and method for conducting academic research. This book is truly the result of Dr. McGinnis' support, inspiration, and direction.

My deep gratitude also goes to Dr. Leslie Saxon, my syntax professor, and committee member. One great memory of my UVic life is that every meeting with Leslie was so supportive, encouraging, and insightful.

My heartfelt gratitude goes to Dr. Catherine Léger, committee member for my graduate study. Dr. Léger's great work and input, her thoughts, questions, and suggestions, make an important part of this book.

My sincere thanks go to Dr. Tsung Cheng Lin. As an influential expert in Chinese linguistics and literature, Dr. Lin gives me great support and valuable direction in writing this book.

Finally, my warmest appreciation goes to Dr. Niina Zhang. Dr. Zhang is not only the external examining member of this research, but also one of the major authors that I learned from and referred to while writing this book. Dr. Zhang's insightful comments and very positive review is a most encouraging and cherished part in writing this book.

Contents

Abbreviations

3	Third person
ACC	Accusative
AGR	Agreement
ASP	Mandarin aspect (perfective) marker
BA	Mandarin *BA*-construction marker
CAUSE	Causative morpheme
CL	Classifier
GEN	Genitive
NAct	Non-active
NOM	Nominative
PASS	Passive
PAST	Past tense
PL	Plural
PROG	Progressive
REN	Japanese *renyoo* morpheme
SG	Singular
STAT	Stative

Chapter 1
Introduction

1.1 The Empirical Domain and Basic Research Questions

This dissertation is a study of the syntax of a construction in Mandarin Chinese, namely, V-V resultatives, or resultative V-V compounds, within the Minimalist framework for generative syntactic theory (Chomsky, 1995, 2000, 2001). Mandarin Chinese (henceforth, Mandarin) is characterized by the widespread use of resultative V-V compounds. A canonical V-V resultative compound, as is shown in (1), is formed by two adjacent verb morphemes. Semantically, this construction roughly conveys a 'cause-result' meaning, with the first verb morpheme (henceforth V_1) indicating a causing event conducted by the subject, and the second verb morpheme (henceforth V_2) the result caused by the V_1 event.

(1) a. John **kan-dao**-le yi-ke shu.
     John cut-fall-ASP a-CL tree
     'John cut down a tree.'

   b. John **zou-lei**-le.
     John walk-be.tired-ASP
     'John got tired from walking.'

In a canonical V-V resultative compound, V_1 can be a transitive verb, as shown in (1a) and (2a), or it can be an intransitive verb, as in (1b) and (2b). V_2 is normally an unaccusative verb,[1] as the examples in (1) and (2) indicate.

---

[1] In generative linguistics, unaccusative verbs normally refer to intransitive verbs whose subjects are not semantic agents, but experiencers or themes of the events denoted by the verbs. Unaccusative verbs in Mandarin conform to this description.

J. Liu, *The Syntax of V-V Resultatives in Mandarin Chinese*,
https://doi.org/10.1007/978-981-33-6846-0_1

(2) a. John **da-si**-le   na-zhi laohu.
　　　John beat-die-ASP that-CL tiger
　　　'John beat and killed that tiger.'

　　b. John **ku-xing**-le.
　　　John cry-be.awake-ASP
　　　'John cried and as a result got awake.'

Based on whether V_2 is predicated of the subject, or of the theme object, V-V resultatives have two subclasses: object-oriented, in which V_2 is predicated of the theme object, as in (3a), and subject-oriented, in which V_2 is predicated of the subject of the clause, as in (3b).[2] In (3a), V_2 *kai* 'open' denotes the resultant state of the object *men* 'door', and it bears no thematic relation to the subject *John*; in contrast, V_2 *bao* 'be full' in (3b) denotes the state of the subject *John*.

(3) a. Object-oriented V-V resultative
　　　John **tui-kai**-le   men.
　　　John push-open-ASP door
　　　'John pushed the door open.'

　　b. Subject-oriented V-V resultative
　　　John **chi-bao**-le.
　　　John eat-be.full-ASP
　　　'John got full from eating.'

As indicated above, in this study, I call these constructions V-V resultatives. Following the literature (e.g., Cheng & Huang, 1994; Y. Li, 1990, 1993; Wang, 2010), I also call them *V-V resultative compounds* when it is more appropriate to use this term in certain contexts. But note that the term *compound* used in this study does not have any theoretical or analytical implication—particularly, it does not reflect any theoretical assumptions about the generation of these constructions. Following Harley (2009), I simply assume that a compound is a morphologically complex form identified as word-sized by its syntactic and phonological behavior and which contains two (or more) roots.

---

[2]V-V resultatives in Mandarin can be divided into different subclasses, as having been discussed in the literature (cf. Cheng & Huang, 1994; Lau & Lee, 2015; Zhang, 2001). For example, according to whether there is a thematic relation between V1 and the theme object of the compound, Zhang (2001) divides these constructions into two groups: transitive resultative constructions, where V1 thematically selects the theme object (ia), and intransitive resultative constructions, where there is no such relation between V1 and the theme object (ib).

(i) a. John **tui-kai**-le   men.
　　　John push-open-ASP door
　　　'John pushed that door open.'

　　b. John **ku-shi**-le   maojin.
　　　John cry-be.wet-ASP towel
　　　'John cried and as a result got the towel wet.'

Crosslinguistically, resultative constructions occupy an important place in current linguistic theory due to their potential to illuminate the nature of the relationship between compositional semantics and syntax. In the literature on Mandarin, V-V resultative constructions have been one of the most studied topics over the past decades (Cheng & Huang, 1994; Cheng, Huang, & Tang, 1997; Fan, 2013; Gu, 1992; Huang, 1992, 2006; Y. Li, 1990, 1993, 1995, 1998, 1999, 2005; Lin, 2004; H. Liu, 2004; Sybesma, 1992, 1999; Wang, 2010; Wu, 2003; Zhang, 2001, to list some of these studies). Despite the extensive discussion in previous studies, however, certain fundamental properties of these constructions are still controversial. Among the various aspects that have been discussed in the literature, the present study particularly focuses on three issues: the generation of the resultative compounds, the syntactic structure of V-V resultatives, and their alternation properties.

The first issue I investigate is the generation of resultative V-V compounds. While V-V resultatives in Mandarin have been heavily studied, the issue of their generation is largely an assumption—rather than a proper research topic—in previous studies. Regarding the generation of morphologically complex words, two competing approaches have been developed in the field of generative linguistics: the lexicalist approach, which argues that complex words are generated in the lexicon, and the syntactic approach, which argues that complex words are formed in syntax. Previous studies disagree on the generation of V-V resultative compounds in Mandarin. Y. Li (2005), for example, argues that they are generated in the lexicon, entering syntax as single words, while some other authors (e.g., H. Liu, 2004; Wang, 2010; Zhang, 2001) assume that they are formed in syntax. The first research question of the present study is:

(I).   In which component of the grammar and with what mechanisms are Mandarin resultative V-V compounds generated?

My second focus is the syntactic structure of V-V resultatives. In this study, I explore an event-based approach to this issue. In current generative linguistics, the syntactic representation of semantic event structure has become the mainstream approach to argument structure (cf. Marantz, 2013), which I call the *event-mapping approach* in this study. Under this approach, the verbal/predicate semantics is decomposed into an event structure, which is represented by the syntactic structure. While it is generally agreed that the semantics/syntax interface is mediated by the event structure, researchers disagree on how exactly syntax reflects and represents the event structure. One stream of thought, the so-called *isomorphism hypothesis* (cf. Lin, 2004), posits that syntax precisely mirrors the event structure through a correspondence relation between syntactic verbal projections (*v*Ps) and (sub)events (e.g., Ramchand, 2008; Ritter & Rosen, 2000; Travis, 2010). Other authors (e.g., Marantz, 2013; Pylkkänen, 2008), in contrast, argue that the correspondence between the semantic event structure and the syntactic argument structure is not a straightforward one. Given this background, my second research question is:

(II).   What is the syntactic structure of V-V resultatives from an event-mapping approach?

The third focus of the present study is the alternation properties of V-V resultatives. One property of resultative V-V compounds is that a small number of them can appear in a variety of argument structures. Notably, when appearing in alternative argument structures, these resultative compounds demonstrate complex properties, many of which remain controversial in previous analyses. For example, the subject-oriented V-V resultative *he-zui* 'drink-be drunk' is normally used as an intransitive predicate, as in (4a). Alternatively, at least for some speakers, this compound can also be used as a transitive, as in (4b). Notably, in the alternative transitive use, as is shown in (4b-c), the subject is under certain restrictions, the nature of which is still unclear.

(4) a. Intransitive use
    John **he-zui**-le.
    John drink-be.drunk-ASP
    'John drank and got drunk.'

  b. Transitive use
    na ping jiu **he-zui**-le   John.
    that bottle wine drink-be.drunk-ASP John
    'That bottle of wine got John drunk.'

  c. Transitive use
    *yumende xinqing **he-zui**-le   John.
    depressed mood   drink-be.drunk-ASP John
    Intended meaning: 'The depressed feeling made John drunk from drinking.'

In addition to the puzzling properties like the subject restriction in alternative uses, some fundamental issues regarding the alternation of resultative V-V compounds have not been addressed. For example, why do only a very small number of resultative V-V compounds have alternative uses, while the majority do not? For the alternating compounds, what allows them to alternate? Why do the alternative uses of some resultative V-V compounds tend to be marginal? Moreover, so far there is no well-grounded categorization system for the alternations, and the descriptive generalizations are still unclear. Based on these controversial issues, the third research question of the present study is:

(III).   How can a unified and principled account for the properties of the alternations of
         V-V resultatives be provided?

1.2   Arguments and Proposals: Preview

1.2.1   The Generation of V-V Resultative Compounds

In this study, I propose a syntactic analysis of the generation of the resultative compounds. Within the framework of Distributed Morphology (Halle & Marantz,

1993), Marantz (2000, 2007) proposes that complex words are formed in two syntactic domains: the inner domain (below the first merged categorizing head little x), or the outer domain (above this little x), and that complex words formed in the two domains demonstrate different properties. Adopting this inner versus outer domain hypothesis for the formation of complex words, I investigate the generation of resultative V-V compounds by comparing them with another type of V-V compounds in Mandarin, namely parallel V-V compounds. Resultative and parallel V-V compounds, while superficially similar, possess systematically different properties, including compositional versus idiosyncratic meanings, different potential for nominalization, free versus bound component morphemes, productivity versus semi-productivity, and different adverbial modification properties. I show that all these contrasting properties can find a natural account under the inner versus outer domain hypothesis. Based on this, I propose that parallel V-V compounds are formed in the inner domain, in which the two acategorical roots ($\sqrt{}_1 + \sqrt{}_2$) combine first to form a root complex, and then merge with little v; in contrast, resultative V-V compounds are formed in the outer domain, by combining two categorized verbs (vP_1 and vP_2).

1.2.2 The Syntactic Structure of V-V Resultatives

Despite the fact that the event-mapping approach has become the mainstream approach to syntactic structure in current linguistic theories, studies that systematically and explicitly apply this approach to the syntactic structure of V-V resultatives in Mandarin are few in the literature. Lin's (2004) widely cited work is the only such study, to my knowledge. Lin proposes an isomorphism analysis, and claims that the two types of V-V resultatives in Mandarin, object-oriented and subject-oriented V-V resultatives, have a unified semantic event structure and syntactic structure. Specifically, Lin argues that the event structure of the two types of V-V resultatives consists of three subevents (activity, change of state, and final state), and correspondingly their syntactic structure contains three vPs (v_{DO}, v_{BECOME}, and v_{BE}), with each vP realizing one subevent.

In contrast to Lin's analysis, using adverbs as probes to test the syntactic structure, the present study makes the following proposal: while semantically V-V resultatives can be analyzed as composed of three subevents (activity, change of state, and final state), the syntax does not generate three vPs in representing their event structure. That is, the isomorphism hypothesis does not hold. Specifically, for object-oriented resultatives, their syntactic structure contains two vPs: one conveys the interpreted meaning of CAUSE, which I label as $v_{CAUSE}P$, and the other the meaning BECOME, which I label as $v_{BECOME}P$; for subject-oriented resultatives, their syntactic structure only contains a $v_{BECOME}P$. That is, object-oriented resultatives have the canonical structure of transitive causatives, while subject-oriented resultatives are intransitive unaccusative predicates.

1.2.3   The Alternation Properties of V-V Resultatives

My analysis of the alternation properties of V-V resultatives crucially invokes my analysis of the syntactic structures of object-oriented and subject-oriented resultatives—that is, these two types of resultative constructions have different structures. Most previous analyses treat all Mandarin resultative constructions as having the same syntactic structure (e.g., Y. Li, 1990, 1993; Lin, 2004; Wang, 2010). From this perspective, there is no categorical difference between the alternations of different resultative V-V compounds, and the alternations are generally viewed as the idiosyncratic property of particular V-V compounds. Therefore in previous studies, the alternations seem largely arbitrary. However, from the perspective of my analysis that the two subclasses of V-V resultatives have different syntactic structures, a substantial difference among their alternative uses appears immediately. Because the two subtypes of V-V resultatives fall into two categories—causatives (object-oriented resultatives), and unaccusatives (subject-oriented resultatives)—their alternations are of different natures: decausativization of causatives (object-oriented resultatives), and causativization of unaccusatives (subject-oriented resultatives). On the basis of this causativization versus decausativization categorization system, I further propose that most of the properties of these alternations arise from two sources: first, the distinctive semantic and syntactic properties of the two types of resultative constructions—particularly the subject-oriented resultatives—and secondly, the Direct Causation Condition on the subject in causative constructions.

1.3   Theoretical Assumptions

The general theoretical background for the present study is the Minimalist Program for syntactic theory (Chomsky, 1995, 2000, 2001), supplemented with the architectural assumptions of Distributed Morphology (Halle & Marantz, 1993; Marantz, 1997), which are sketched below.

The Minimalist Program (MP, henceforth) hypothesizes that the human language faculty interfaces with the Articulatory-Perceptual (A-P) system and Conceptual-Intentional (C-I) systems through two levels of representation: Phonetic Form (PF) and Logical Form (LF) respectively. MP assumes that the language faculty comprises a lexicon and a computational/derivational system. The lexicon specifies the items that enter into the computational system, and lexical items are bundles of syntactic/semantic features. The computational system arranges these items to form a pair containing a PF object and an LF object, which is sent to the two interface levels for phonological realization and semantic interpretation.

To be very brief, a typical derivation in MP is as follows. Once the bundles of syntactic/semantic features associated with lexical items enter the computational system, syntactic operations, including Merge, Agree, and Move, manipulate and link them to form larger units. In due course of this computational process, a derived structure is shipped to the two interfaces (LF and PF) for interpretation, and this is the point at which the derivation to PF splits off from the syntax.

Particularly, MP hypothesizes that the derivations proceed phase by phase. That is, rather than for a whole clause to be interpreted, syntactic structures are interpreted cyclically, within syntactic domains called *phases*. When a phase is completed in the course of the derivation, it is transferred to the two interfaces for interpretation (Chomsky, 2000).[3] Note that one property of phases is that, once the derivation within a given phase has been completed, the domain of the phase, i.e., the complement of the phase head, becomes impenetrable to further syntactic operations. This is the Phase Impenetrability Condition. The syntactic objects that qualify for phases include DP, vP, and CP.

In addition to MP, another assumption of the present study is the theory of Distributed Morphology (Halle & Marantz, 1993; Marantz, 1997). Distributed Morphology (DM, henceforth) proposes an architecture of grammar in which a single generative system, the syntax, is responsible both for word structure and phrase structure. In other words, DM rejects the existence of a generative lexicon in the architecture of grammar, and argues that all composition of morphemes occurs in the syntax as a result of syntactic combination. DM assumes that syntax manipulates abstract feature bundles into a hierarchical tree structure, and the identifiable morphemes are the realizations of the terminal nodes of this structure.

Within the DM framework, words are not atomic elements for syntactic computation, nor do they have a special status in syntactic derivation. As Marantz (2000) puts it, in DM, complex words, for example *nationalization*, have no essential difference from sentences like *The cat is on the mattress* in terms of syntactic generation. Instead, DM contends that the traditional terms for sentence elements, such as noun, verb, and adjective are essentially derivative from more basic syntactic elements. DM hypothesizes two classes of terminal nodes: roots, which are acategorial, and functional elements of various kinds, such as categorizing heads little x (including v, n, and a), which categorize a root (or a larger structure) as a verb, a noun, or an adjective. Roots are categorized by merging with a categorizing functional head.

1.4 Outline of the Dissertation

The dissertation is structured as follows. After this chapter of introduction, I first consider the generation of resultative V-V compounds in Chap. 2. In Chap. 2, I first review a key theoretical assumption of my analysis of this issue, Marantz's (2000) inner versus outer generation hypothesis. Next I introduce another type of V-V compounds, the parallel V-V compounds. Then, after briefly reviewing some previous studies on this issue, I present the contrasting properties of the two types

---

[3]Note that, different from Chomsky (2000), Chomsky (2001) proposes that the shipment of the domain of a phase for interpretation occurs at the completion of the next phase. As this is not crucial for my analysis, I will follow Chomsky (2000).

of V-V compounds, and demonstrate how the inner versus outer domain hypothesis captures these contrasting properties, thus arguing for my analysis of the generation of resultative V-V compounds.

Chapter 3 presents my analysis of the argument structure of V-V resultatives. This chapter contains two major parts. I devote the first part to a comprehensive review of my theoretical approach, the event-mapping approach to argument structure. Highlights of this section include the contrast between lexicalist and syntactic approaches to argument structure, the autonomy of syntactic structures from verbal meanings, the decomposition of verbal/predicate semantics in the form of event structure, and several theories of the semantics/syntax interface as mediated by event structure. In the second part, I present my analysis. The main feature of this section is an argument that a close examination of the adverbial modification properties of the two types of V-V resultatives can provide insights into the syntactic structure of V-V resultatives in Mandarin. I will show that these adverbial modification properties point to two conclusions: first, the isomorphism analysis proposed in Lin (2004) does not hold; second, object-oriented and subject-oriented V-V resultatives have different syntactic structures, despite their seemingly similar surface forms and their common 'cause-result' semantics.

In Chap. 4 I turn my focus to the subject properties of V-V resultatives and their alternation properties. In this chapter, I first show that the subject in object-oriented resultatives is an external argument, while it is a derived subject (i.e. not an external argument) in subject-oriented resultatives. I thus provide further support for the analysis that the two types of resultatives have different syntactic structures. Then, based on this 'different-structure' analysis, I propose a 'causativization versus decausativization' approach to the alternative uses of these resultatives. I then further demonstrate that this approach, together with the Direct Causation Condition on the subject in causatives, can account for relevant alternation properties satisfactorily.

Finally Chap. 5 concludes the study. In this chapter, I briefly review the main arguments, and discuss the contribution of this work to the field. I also point out some relevant questions for future study.

References

Cheng, L., & Huang, C.-T. (1994). On the argument structure of resultative compounds. In Y. Chen, J. Ovid, & L. Tzeng (Eds.), *In honour of William S.-Y. Wang: Interdisciplinary studies in language and language change* (pp. 187–221). Taiwan: Pyramid.

Cheng, L.-S., Huang, C.-T., Li, Y.-H., & Tang, C.-C. (1997). Causative compounds across Chinese dialects: A study of Cantonese, Mandarin and Taiwanese. *Chinese Languages and Linguistics, 4,* 199–224.

Chomsky, N. (1995). *Minimalist program.* Cambridge, MA: MIT Press.

Chomsky, N. (2000). Minimalist inquires. In R. Martin, M. Michaels, & J. Uriagereka (Eds.), *Step by step: Essays on minimalist syntax in honor of Howard Lasnik* (pp. 89–155). Cambridge, MA: MIT Press.

Chomsky, N. (2001). Derivation by phase. In M. Kenstowicz (Ed.), *Ken Hale: A life in language* (pp. 1–52). Cambridge, MA: MIT Press.

Fan, S. (2013). Argument structure in Mandarin Chinese: A lexical-syntactic perspective. Doctoral dissertation, Universidad Autónoma de Madrid, Spain.

Gu, Y. (1992). The syntax of resultative and causative compounds in Chinese. Doctoral dissertation, Cornell University.

Halle, M., & Marantz, A. (1993). Distributed morphology and the pieces of inflection. In K. Hale & S. Keyser (Eds.), *The view from building 20* (pp. 111–176). Cambridge, MA: MIT Press.

Harley, H. (2009). Compounding in distributed morphology. In R. Lieber & P. Štekauer (Eds.), *The Oxford handbook of compounding* (pp. 129–144). Oxford: Oxford University Press.

Huang, C.-T. (1992). Complex predicates in control. In R. Larson, U. Lahiri, S. Iatridou, & J. Higginbotham (Eds.), *Control and grammar* (pp. 109–147). Dordrecht: Kluwer.

Huang, C.-T. (2006). Resultatives and unaccusatives: A parametric view. *Bulletin of the Chinese Linguistic Society of Japan, 253,* 1–43.

Lau, Y., & Lee, Y. (2015). A comparative study on Mandarin and Cantonese resultative verb compounds. In *29th Pacific Asia Conference on Language, Information and Computation* (pp. 231–239).

Li, Y. (1990). On V-V compounds in Chinese. *Natural Language & Linguistic Theory, 8,* 177–207.

Li, Y. (1993). Structural head and aspectuality. *Language, 69,* 480–504.

Li, Y. (1995). The thematic hierarchy and causativity. *Natural Language & Linguistic Theory, 13,* 255–282.

Li, Y. (1998). Chinese resultative constructions and the Uniformity of Theta Assignment Hypothesis. In J. Packard (Ed.), *New approaches to Chinese word formation* (pp. 285–310). Berlin: Mouton De Gruyter.

Li, Y. (1999). Cross-componential causativity. *Natural Language & Linguistic Theory, 17,* 445–497.

Li, Y. (2005). X^0: A theory of the morphology-syntax interface. Cambridge, MA: MIT Press.

Lin, J. (2004). Event structure and the encoding of arguments: The syntax of the Mandarin and English verb phrase. Doctoral dissertation, Massachusetts Institute of Technology.

Liu, H. (2004). Complex predicates in Mandarin Chinese: Three types of *Bu-Yu* structures. Doctoral dissertation, University of California.

Marantz, A. (1997). No escape from syntax: Don't try morphological analysis in the privacy of your own lexicon. In A. Dimitriadis & L. Siegel (Eds.), *University of Pennsylvania Working Papers in Linguistics, vol. 4. Proceedings of the 21st Annual Penn Linguistics Colloquium* (pp. 201–225).

Marantz, A. (2000). *Words.* Massachusetts Institute of Technology: Unpublished ms.

Marantz, A. (2013). Verbal argument structure: Events and participants. *Lingua, 130,* 152–168.

Marantz, A., et al. (2007). Phases and words. In S. Choe (Ed.), *Phases in the theory of grammar* (pp. 191–222). Seoul: Dong In.

Pylkkänen, L. (2008). *Introducing arguments.* Cambridge, MA: MIT Press.

Ramchand, G. (2008). *Verb meaning and the Lexicon: A First-phase syntax.* Cambridge: Cambridge University Press.

Ritter, E., & Rosen, S. (2000). Event structure and ergativity. In C. Tenny & J. Pustejovsky (Eds.), *Events as grammatical objects: The converging perspectives of lexical semantics and syntax* (pp. 187–238). Stanford: CSLI Publications.

Sybesma, R. (1992). Causatives and accomplishments: The case of Chinese ba. Doctoral dissertation, Leiden University.

Sybesma, R. (1999). *The Mandarin VP.* Dordrecht & Boston: Kluwer.

Travis, L. (2010). *Inner aspect: The articulation of VP.* Dordrecht: Springer.

Wang, C. (2010). The microparametric syntax of resultatives in Chinese languages. Doctoral dissertation, New York University.

Wu, C. (2003). Some notes on resultative constructions: On flip-flop constructions. In *McGill Working Papers in Linguistics* (Vol. 18, pp. 89–125). Montreal: McGill University.

Zhang, N. (2001). The structures of depictive and resultative constructions in Chinese. *ZAS Papers in Linguistics, 22,* 191–221.

Chapter 2
The Generation of Resultative V-V Compounds

2.1 Introduction

In this chapter I address the first fundamental issue of resultative V-V compounds in Mandarin: their generation. To be more specific, I explore in which component of the grammar and with what mechanisms they are generated.

The generation of morphologically complex words has been a central issue in generative linguistics. Two competing approaches have been developed in past decades: the lexicalist approach, which argues that complex words are generated in the lexicon, and the syntactic approach, which argues that complex words, like other complex constructions such as phrases and clauses, are formed in syntax. Previous studies on Mandarin resultative V-V compounds disagree on the locus and mechanisms of their generation; while some studies (e.g., Cheng & Huang, 1994; Y. Li, 2005) argue they are formed in the lexicon, others (e.g., Lin, 2004; H. Liu, 2004; Wang, 2010; Zhang, 2001) assume that they are generated in syntax.

Within the framework of Distributed Morphology (Halle & Marantz, 1993, and subsequent works), which posits that complex words are formed in syntax, Marantz (2000, 2007) further proposes that, in forming complex words, morphemes that combine with a lexical root can be generated in two different places: below the first merged category-defining head (little x), which is called *the inner domain*, or above this head, which is called *the outer domain*. According to this hypothesis, morphemes merged in these two domains demonstrate systematically different properties.

Adopting this inner versus outer domain hypothesis for the formation of complex words, I examine and compare two types of V-V compounds in Mandarin in this chapter. Besides resultative V-V compounds, as exemplified in (1a), Mandarin has another type of V-V compounds, the so-called *parallel V-V compounds* (Li & Thompson, 1981), the defining character of which is that the two component morphemes have similar meanings. A typical parallel V-V compound is exemplified in (1b).

(1) a. Resultative V-V compound
    John **kan-dao**-le   yi-ke shu.
    John cut-fall-ASP a-CL tree
    'John cut down a tree.'

  b. Parallel V-V compound
    John hen **xiang-nian**   jiaren.
    John very think.about-miss family
    'John missed his family very much.'

A closer inspection indicates that resultative and parallel V-V compounds, while superficially similar, demonstrate systematically different properties. Importantly, the properties of these two types of V-V compounds fit perfectly into the inner versus outer domain hypothesis for complex words formation: parallel V-V compounds conform to the characteristics of words formed in the inner domain; resultative V-V compounds, in contrast, demonstrate properties of words formed in the outer domain.

The contrasting properties of resultative and parallel V-V compounds form the main argument for my analysis of the generation of Mandarin resultative V-V compounds. I argue that parallel V-V compounds are formed in the inner domain, in which the two acategorical roots ($\sqrt{}_1$ and $\sqrt{}_2$) combine first to form a root complex, which then merges with the functional categorizing head little v (2a); resultative V-V compounds, in contrast, are formed by combining two categorized verbs (vP_1 and vP_2), as shown in (2b). I thus propose a syntactic analysis of the generation of Mandarin resultative V-V compounds.

(2) a. Formation of parallel V-V compounds   b. Formation of resultative V-V compounds

Note that, in (2a), in forming a parallel V-V compound, the root complex ($\sqrt{}_1 +$ $\sqrt{}_2$) merges with little v. In contrast, in forming a resultative V-V compound (2b), each of the two roots merges with a little v to form two verbs first, then two verbs combine to form a resultative V-V compound.[1]

This chapter is organized as follows. In Sect. 2.2, I sketch the contrasts between the lexical and syntactic approaches to the formation of complex morphemes, to provide a general context for my analysis. In Sect. 2.3, I review some evidence for the core theoretical assumption of my analysis, Marantz's (2000) inner versus outer generation hypothesis. Section 2.4 reviews a major previous study of the generation of resultative V-V compounds in Mandarin, Y. Li's (2005) analysis. After this preparatory work, in Sect. 2.5, I present my analysis of the generation of Mandarin resultative V-V compounds. In this section, I first introduce the parallel V-V compounds, and

---

[1] For the purpose of this chapter I will just focus on the domain of the generation of resultative V-V compounds (as well as parallel V-V compounds), and will neglect the specific structural relation between the two vPs. In my analysis of the syntactic structure of resultative V-V compounds in Chap. 3, I will provide a more detailed syntactic structure for the resultative V-V compounds.

list the contrasting properties of the two types of V-V compounds (Sect. 2.5.1), and then I demonstrate how the inner versus outer generation hypothesis captures these contrasting properties (Sect. 2.5.2). Section 2.6 concludes this chapter.

2.2 Lexicalist Versus Syntactic Approaches to Word Formation

2.2.1 The Lexicalist Approach

Generally speaking, the lexicalist approach to the formation of complex words postulates that, while some complex morphology, particularly inflectional morphology, is generated in syntax, certain complex morphology, such as derivational morphology, is stored in the lexicon (e.g., Chomsky, 1970; Dubinsky & Simango, 1996; Wasow, 1977). Chomsky (1970) proposes that derived nominalizations, like *laugh-ter*, *marriage*, and *construc-tion*, are stored in the lexicon, while gerunds are generated in syntax. This analysis postulates a division between words stored in the lexicon and words formed in syntax, which was further developed in many influential works in the following decades (e.g., Anderson, 1982; Aronoff, 1976; Bresnan & Mchombo, 1995; Di Sciullo & Williams, 1987; Lieber, 1980), and became a major assumption of many studies.

The lexicalist approach is based on the fundamental assumption that there exists an autonomous, pre-syntactic component in grammar, the lexicon, which stores and generates words, and feeds them into the syntax for computation. Briefly speaking, this approach generally comprises the following assumptions: (i) besides a list of underived lexical entries, the lexicon also contains a computational mechanism for the formation of (certain) complex words; (ii) words formed in the lexicon are built out of different elements from units formed in syntax: the morphological constituents of words are lexical categories (stems and affixes), whereas the syntactic constituents of phrases have words as the minimal, unanalyzable units; (iii) the lexical operations that generate words (such as suffixation, prefixation, and compounding) are independent of, and different from, syntactic operations; iv) words generated in the lexicon enter into syntax as unanalyzable atomic units, and the syntax has no access to the internal structure of words—the so-termed Principle of Lexical Integrity (Bresnan & Mchombo, 1995; Di Sciullo & Williams, 1987; Lapointe, 1980).

As just mentioned, the lexicalist approach posits that complex words are formed in two different components of the grammar, lexicon and syntax. The empirical basis for this claim is that, the two canonical categories of morphology, inflectional and derivational, demonstrate different properties, which are said to follow from, and reflect, the different properties of these two components of the grammar (lexicon and syntax) (e.g., Svenonius, 2005; Travis, 2000; Wasow, 1977). Among these different properties, one primary example is the compositional versus idiosyncratic semantics of the two types of complex words. That is, while inflectional morphology shows regular and compositional semantics, the meanings of derivational morphology are sometimes noncompositional and idiosyncratic. Another major difference involves the productivity of the two types of complex words: the generation of inflected forms is usually highly productive, whereas the generation of derived forms is irregular and not fully productive. Some of the contrasts traditionally associated with forms generated in the lexicon and in syntax are summarized in (3).

(3)

Complex forms generated in the lexicon	Complex forms generated in the syntax
Idiosyncratic and noncompositional meaning	Compositional and predictable meaning
Can change lexical category	Does not change category (in most cases)
Memorized and listed in lexicon	Constructed in grammar
Not fully productive	Fully productive
Cannot interact with syntactic rules	Can interact with syntactic rules

2.2.2   Word Formation in Distributed Morphology: A Syntactic Approach

As mentioned earlier, a syntactic approach to morphology aims to provide a syntactic account for the formation of complex words (e.g., Borer, 2005; Embick, 2004, 2010; Halle & Marantz, 1993; Marantz, 1997). Distributed Morphology is such a framework. In order to compare it with the lexicalist approach presented above, I briefly expand my review of DM here.

Fundamentally, DM rejects the existence of a generative lexicon component in the architecture of grammar, and maintains that syntax is the only generative engine, and that composition and combination of morphemes occurs in the syntax. In DM, words are not atomic elements for syntactic computation, but are often syntactically derived from more basic units corresponding to morphemes. DM hypothesizes two main types of atomic units in the syntactic derivation: lexical roots, and bundles of syntactic/semantic features. DM assumes that, just like larger syntactic units such as phrases and sentences, complex words are also made up of syntactic atoms via syntactic mechanisms.

Within the DM framework, Marantz (2000) further proposes that the merge of functional morphemes in syntax occurs in two different domains—below or above the first merged functional categorizing head (little x). I adopt this hypothesis in my analysis of the generation of Mandarin V-V resultatives, and in the next section, I review this hypothesis in more detail.

2.3   The Inner Versus Outer Domain Hypothesis for Complex Word Formation

2.3.1   The Inner Versus Outer Domain Hypothesis

According to Marantz (2000, 2007), one domain for the merge of the syntactic nodes underlying functional morphemes is the local domain of a lexical root, the so-called *inner domain*, in which a morpheme (head) merges before a functional categorizing head (little x) combines with the root. The other domain, the so-called *outer domain*, is outside the domain of the first merged functional categorizing head little x. The mechanism of morpheme attachment in the inner and the outer domains is as schematized in (4). In the inner domain (4a), a head merges with a lexical root below the first merged categorizing head little x. In the outer domain (4b), in contrast, the head corresponding to a functional morpheme is merged above the xP—rather than directly merging with the lexical root.

(4)   a.   b.

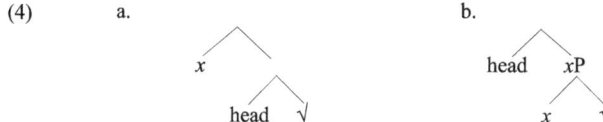

While traditionally the domain of the root is called the *inner domain*, and the domain outside the root domain, the *outer domain*, it should be noted that the term *outer domain* might be misleading, as a complex word formed in the so-termed *outer domain* does not just contain the morphemes above the functional little x, but also the morphemes corresponding to the categorizing head little x as well as the lexical root, which belong to the inner domain. For the sake of an easy reference, in the rest of this chapter, I will refer to this inner versus outer domain hypothesis for complex word formation simply as the *two-domain hypothesis*.

A major feature of the two-domain hypothesis is that it emphasizes the role of the syntactic locality domain in determining the properties of complex words. Marantz argues that the two different domains play a crucial role in producing the different properties of different types of complex words: a complex word generated close to the root demonstrates traditionally lexical, idiosyncratic properties; a complex word generated in the outer domain demonstrates traditionally syntactic, paradigmatic properties. Marantz argues that the different properties traditionally associated with derivational and inflectional morphemes, which have been attributed to their generation in two different grammatical components, actually arise from their generation in different syntactic domains. As Marantz states, word formation is "all about locality […] and information encapsulation within syntactically defined domains" (2000, p. 4).

Furthermore, Marantz argues that the locality constraint that produces the different properties of complex morphemes formed in different domains follows from two fundamental mechanisms: the special properties of the roots with regard to their semantic interpretation, and the phase-based cyclical nature of syntactic computation. I present this point below.

Within the DM framework, it is assumed that a lexical root, after merging with the categorizing head, will be semantically interpreted. Particularly, it has been argued that the root domain, i.e. the inner domain, demonstrates unique properties in semantic interpretation—that is, idiosyncratic meanings may arise (cf. Anagnostopoulou & Samioti, 2014; Arad, 2003; Ramchand, 2008). To be more specific, root semantic interpretation demonstrates the following two properties.

The first property is that roots are associated with non-grammatical, 'encyclopedic' semantic content, i.e. knowledge of the world, not just grammatical meanings. Ramchand (2008), for example, views the inner domain as the interface between the encyclopedic conception and syntactic representation. Marantz (2007) argues that the meaning contribution of a root is never independently realized, since the objects of interpretation are phases, not roots. A root can have particular meanings and a variety of uses, which can be different from speaker to speaker.

The second property is that root meanings—unlike the compositional semantic features expressed through syntactic combination—do not decompose. Marantz (2000) states that the internal semantic structure of roots, unlike the internal structure of sentences, cannot be decomposed or composed in the grammar. Marantz cites the example of the word *cake* from Fodor and Lepore (1998) to demonstrate this. A semantic property of a *cake* is that it is baked to eat, but the meaning of *cake* does not decompose into making, baking, and eating. The two-domain hypothesis posits that it is the idiosyncratic properties assigned to the elements in the root domain that underlie the idiosyncratic semantics typically associated with derivational morphemes. This analysis is thus different from the lexicalist analysis that the semantic idiosyncrasy of derivational morphemes is due to their generation in the lexicon.

In addition to the unique semantic properties of the root domain, the contrasting properties of morphemes merged in the two locality domains also follow from the architecture of the grammar, and the cyclic nature of syntactic computation. DM posits that syntactic structures are first generated in syntax, and then are shipped to PF and LF for phonetic and semantic interpretation. As noted in Chap. 1, MP hypothesizes that the syntactic derivation and transfer to PF and LF are conducted in a cyclic manner, based on the phase domain. Specifically, once a phase head is merged, its complement domain is shipped to PF and LF for phonological and semantic interpretation. Note that one entailment of this grammatical architecture and the phase-based spell-out mechanism is that once a (part of the) structure is spelled out, its semantic interpretation (and pronunciation as well) is fixed and cannot be altered by later operations. Given the assumption that the first categorizing head little x also functions as a phase head (see Marantz, 2000, 2007), this means that once the little x is merged, the root or a more complex constituent formed by inner affixation will be shipped off to PF and LF for pronunciation and interpretation, the result of which is that the meaning of the lexical root or root complex will be fixed. This also means that whatever comes next in the course of the derivation will not merge directly with the root, but will combine with a categorized phrase, such as a *v*P containing a verb derived from the combination of the root and *v*, nor can further derivation alter the interpretation of this verb. Due to this property, complex words formed across a categorizing head can only reflect the fixed semantics of the categorized root, thus demonstrating semantic compositionality.

I demonstrate this two-domain hypothesis by citing the example of Chichewa stative and passive morphemes (Dubinsky & Simango, 1996; Marantz, 1997, 2000). Chichewa has two categories of verb-based adjectives, which are formed by combining a verbal stem and one of two passive suffixes, *ika* and *idwa*. When *ika* attaches to a verb, a stative passive is formed, as in (5a); when *idwa* attaches to a verb, an eventive passive is formed (5b).

(5) a. chimanga chi-ku-gul-**ika**   ku-msika.
      corn   AGR-PROG-buy-STAT at-market
      'Corn is cheap at the market.'
      [idiomatic reading of 'buy' in the context of STAT]

   b. chimanga chi-ku-gul-**idwa**   ku-msika.
      corn   AGR-PROG-buy-PASS at-market
      'Corn is being bought at the market.'
      [no idiomatic reading, and not possible with passive]

                             (Marantz, 2000, p. 4)

Notably, the stative and eventive passives demonstrate systematically different properties. First, stative passives can carry idiosyncratic meanings not found in the active counterpart, while eventive passives lack this property; second, while the stative morpheme cannot attach outside an applicative or causative morpheme, the eventive passive can; third, while the stative passive morpheme can trigger stem allomorphy, the eventive passive morpheme cannot (Dubinsky & Simango, 1996). Marantz (1997, 2000) argues that the different properties of the Chichewa stative versus eventive passive morphemes follow from their generation in different domains. Specifically, for stative passives, the morpheme *ika* attaches below the little *v*; for eventive passives, the morpheme *idwa* attaches above the little *v*.

2.3.2   *The Crosslinguistic Application of the Two-Domain Hypothesis*

In the literature, the two-domain hypothesis for complex word formation has been widely adopted to account for the phenomenon in various languages that some constructions, while superficially similar, nonetheless demonstrate different proper-ties, such as compositional versus idiosyncratic semantics (e.g., Arad, 2003; Basilico, 2008; Bruening, 2014). For example, in Hebrew, a root can combine with various categorizing heads to generate words of various categories and subtypes. As illus-trated in (6), the root *vbxn* can combine with various subtypes of little *v* and little *n* heads.

(6)   *Root*   *little v*   *verbs*

          √bxn   a. CaCaC   baxan 'test, examine'
                    b. hiCCiC   hivxin 'discern'

                      little n   *nouns*

                    c. miCCaC   mivxan 'an exam'
                    d. CoCaC   boxan 'a quiz'
                    e. maCCeCa   mavxena 'a test-tube'

Arad (2003) shows that the root is assigned distinct interpretations in different morphological environments when combining with these different category-determining heads. These interpretations are not predictable from the combination of the root and the word-creating head, as demonstrated in (6). On the other hand, in Hebrew, complex words can also be based on existing words. Importantly, Arad observes that, in this case, the newly formed word must reflect the (root) meaning of this existing word. In keeping with the two-domain hypothesis, Arad provides an account of this semantic contrast between words formed from roots, and words formed from existing words. She proposes that, while the former are formed in the inner domain, the latter are generated by adding a second categorizing head in the outer domain. Based on the Hebrew data, Arad particularly argues that roots are assigned an interpretation in the environment of the first category-assigning head with which they are merged. Once this interpretation is assigned, it is carried along throughout the derivation.

Anagnostopoulou and Samioti (2013) provide another example of the application of this two-domain hypothesis. Anagnostopoulou and Samioti use adjectival participles in Greek to investigate how semantic idiosyncrasy arises in word formation. Greek has two types of verb-based adjectival participles: adjectival participles, which have the form of verb-*tos*, and resultative participles, which have the form of verb-*menos*. Notably, these two types of participles show systematic semantic and syntactic differences. For example, while the -*tos* participles show special meanings, in the sense that they may have a meaning not transparently derived from the meaning of the corresponding verb, resultative -*menos* participles, in contrast, always have a meaning regularly related to the verb meaning. Another contrast is that, while the formation of -*menos* participles is fully productive, there are many gaps in the formation of -*tos* participles. Anagnostopoulou and Samioti (2013) adopt the two-domain hypothesis and propose that -*tos* participles instantiate inner-cycle attachment, as demonstrated in (7a), while -*menos* participles instantiate outer-cycle attachment (7b).

(7)   a.   Root attachment   b. Outer domain attachment

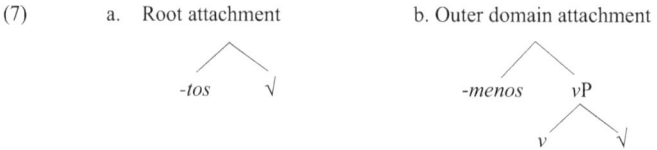

Similarly, Sugimura & Obata (2016) apply this hypothesis to account for the different properties between the two types of *renyoo* forms in Japanese. Japanese

has a conjugational form, the so-called *renyoo*, in which the suffix morpheme *-i* is attached to a root. The *renyoo* forms function either as verbs, as in (8a), or nouns, as in (8b), where the noun is marked with nominative *-ga*.

(7)   a.   Root attachment   b. Outer domain attachment

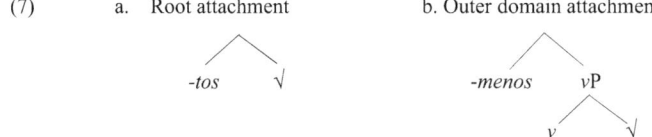

It has been observed that the verbal and nominal *renyoo* forms, despite their surface similarities, demonstrate systematically different properties. In the first place, while *renyoo* verbs retain the core meanings of roots, as shown in (8a) above, *renyoo* nouns, which are marked with the nominative case (NOM), often yield idiosyncratic meanings, as illustrated in (8b). Secondly, *renyoo* verbs are highly productive in that any verb can take the *renyoo* form; *renyoo* nouns, in contrast, are far less productive.

Adopting the two-domain hypothesis, Sugimura & Obata (2016) propose that a *renyoo* noun is formed in the inner domain, by merging a root directly with the categorizer *n*, which is phonologically realized as the *renyoo* morpheme *-i* (9a); on the other hand, a *renyoo* verb is formed by first merging a root with the categorizer *v* and then the REN head, phonologically realized as the *renyoo* morpheme *-i* (9b).

(9)   a. Structure of *renyoo* noun   b. Structure of *renyoo* verb

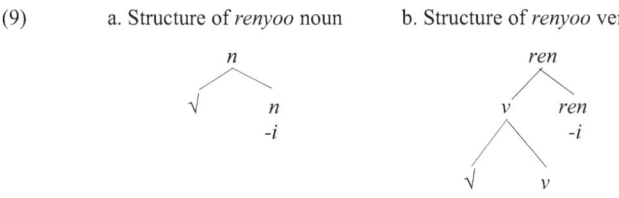

Like the root-based and word-based words in Hebrew, adjectival and resultative participles in Greek, and verbal and nominal *renyoo* forms in Japanese, Mandarin resultative and parallel V-V compounds seem to make a similar case. In Sect. 2.5, I will show that Mandarin resultative and parallel V-V compounds demonstrate systematically different properties, and that these different properties can also be captured with the two-domain hypothesis. First, however, I review some previous studies of the formation of resultative V-V compounds to better contextualize my analysis.

2.4   A Lexicalist Analysis: Y. Li (2005)

The issue of whether Mandarin resultative V-V compounds are generated in the lexicon or in syntax has not received much attention in so far. For most studies of Mandarin V-V resultatives, their generation has been largely a matter of assumption, rather than a subject of investigation. Y. Li (1990, 1993) and C. Li (2008, 2013), for example, assume that resultative V-V compounds are lexical items, and based on this assumption, they propose lexical-semantic analyses of them. Similarly, Chang's (2003, 2007) studies on the linking of arguments to syntax and Cheng & Huang's (1994) analysis of argument structure of resultative V-V compounds in Mandarin both begin from the assumption that these compounds are lexical items, though bearing a more complex event structure than simplex verbs.

In contrast to studies that assume a lexical generation of Mandarin resultative V-V compounds, some other studies, for example H. Liu (2004), Wang (2010), and Zhang (2001), posit that Mandarin resultative V-V compounds are generated in syntax. Notably, in all these studies, the investigation focus is the syntactic structure of resultative V-V constructions—an issue that bears implications for, but is not exactly the same as, the question of where they are generated. For these authors, having presupposed that Mandarin resultative V-V compounds are generated in syntax, their major task is to work out the syntactic structure of this construction. In the three studies mentioned above, for example, the resultative predicate (V_2) is analyzed, variously, as a VP (H. Liu, 2004), a vP (Zhang, 2001), and a CP (Wang, 2010).

Analyses arguing for a syntactic generation of resultative V-V compounds generally propose that they are derived from another resultative construction, the V-*de* construction. In a V-*de* construction, the verb representing the causing event (V_1) is followed by a suffix -*de*, which in turn is followed by a verb phrase indicating the resulting event, in which V_2 is the lexical head. Below, (10a) is an example of a V-V resultative construction, and (10b) is an example of the V-*de* resultative construction.

(10) a. Resultative V-V compound
    Likui **gan-zou**-le   guan-bing.
    Likui chase-leave-ASP government.soldier
    'Likui chased off the soldiers.'

   b. V-*de* resultative construction
    Likui **gan**-de   guan-bing   sichu   bentao.
    Likui chase-DE government.soldier everywhere ran.away
    'Likui chased the soldiers off to all directions.'

In many cases, a V-*de* construction can find a corresponding V-V construction that has a similar meaning (and vice versa), as illustrated by (10a) and (10b). Largely due to this semantic correspondence, some authors have argued for a derivational relation between the two constructions, involving movement of the lower V to combine with the higher V to produce the V-V compound (e.g., Huang, 2006; H. Liu, 2004; Zhang, 2001).

For example, Nishiyama (1998) gives a syntactic analysis of Mandarin V-V resultatives. Nishiyama proposes a double VP structure as in (11b) for Mandarin resultative compounds like (11a), and argues that, in a resultative V-V compound, V_1 is the matrix verb, which is dominated by a vP, and V_2 projects a bare embedded VP.

(11) a. Likui **gan-zou**-le   guan-bing.
Likui chase-leave-ASP government.soldier
'Likui chased off the soldiers.'

b.

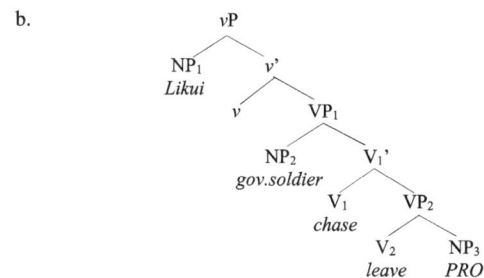

To my knowledge, Y. Li (2005) is the only work that specifically addresses the locus of the generation of Chinese V-V resultative compounds. Y. Li (2005) argues against a syntactic analysis of resultative V-V compounds, and instead proposes that these compounds enter the syntax as single verbs. Y. Li's argument is based on his observation that resultative V-V compounds and V-*de* construction have different syntactic properties that do not obviously follow from movement of the lower V in V-V compounds. The first difference is that, while duration adverbs can occur in V-*de* constructions, modifying V_2, as in (12a), they cannot occur in V-V constructions (12b).

(12) a. Likui lei-de   ku-le   liangtian.
Likui tired-DE cry-ASP two.day
'Likui was so tired that he wept for two days.'

b. *Likui **lei-ku**-le   liangtian.
Likui tired-cry-ASP two.day
Intended meaning: the same as (12a).

The second difference Y. Li claims, which is crucial for his argument, is that these two constructions demonstrate different anaphor binding properties. The V-*de* construction is generally analyzed as biclausal (e.g., Huang, 1992; Y. Li, 1998), predicting that in a V-*de* construction, an anaphor serving as the object of a transitive V_2 can be bound by the local embedded subject, but not by the matrix subject. Y. Li (2005) suggests that one way of testing whether the resultative V-V construction and the V-*de* construction have a parallel structure is to construct a resultative V-V construction in which V_2 is transitive, carrying a theme DP, and then observe the binding possibilities for this DP. Y. Li argues that, if the V-V construction has the same structure with the V-*de* construction, then the theme DP of V_2 in the V-V construction will not allow binding by the matrix subject. The minimal pair Y. Li constructs is (13).[2]

---

[2]Note that the test suggested by Y. Li requires that the second verb (V_2) in the resultative V-V constructions is associated with two arguments, an external argument and a theme object. However, this is unusual for resultative V-V constructions, as normally V_2 in resultative V-V constructions is associated with just one argument, either an external argument or a theme object. In order to construct these testing examples, Y. Li resorts to the *BA* construction. The *BA* construction in

(13) a. Resultative V-V construction

fashi-men$_i$ (nian zhou) ba ren-men$_j$ **nian-wang**-le   gezi$_{i/j}$-de   chengnuo.
priest-pl   recite spell BA people-pl recite-forget-ASP each.own's promise
By reciting spells, the priests$_i$ made people$_j$ forget their$_{i/j}$ own promises.

b. V-*de* construction

fashi-men$_i$ (nian zhou) ba ren-men$_j$ **nian-de   wang**-le   gezi$_{*i/j}$-de   chengnuo.
priest-pl   recite spell BA people-pl recite-DE forget-ASP each.own's promise
By reciting spells, the priests$_i$ made people$_j$ forget their$_{*i/j}$ own promises.

Y. Li notes that, in the V-*de* construction (13b), the anaphoric possessor *gezi-de* 'each own's' contained in the theme DP of V$_2$ *gezi-de chengnuo* 'each own's promise' can only be bound by the post-*BA* DP *ren-men* 'people', that is, by the embedded subject. In the resultative V-V construction (13a), however, the anaphoric possessor in the theme can be bound by either the matrix subject *fashi-men* 'priests', or the causee *ren-men* 'people'. Y. Li argues that the different binding properties demonstrated in (13) not only indicate that resultative V-V constructions and V-*de* constructions have different syntactic structures, but also provide direct evidence that the resultative V-V compound in (13a) is a simplex verb. According to Y. Li, the fact that both the matrix subject and the causee can bind the anaphoric possessor in (13a) indicates that the two verb stems occupy the same binding domain, and therefore must be analyzed as combined into a single syntactic verb.[3]

Y. Li claims that (13a) poses a major challenge for a syntactic analysis of V-V compounds such as that of Nishiyama (1998). On the one hand, if V$_2$ is analyzed as projecting its own verb phrase, there is no way to avoid representing the projection of V$_2$ as anything less than *v*P, as V$_2$ *wang* '*forget*' introduces its own thematic subject *ren-men* 'people'. On the other hand, if V$_2$ is dominated by its own *v*P, this *v*P should be the binding domain for *gezi-de* 'each own's', and it would be difficult to explain why the matrix subject can also bind *gezi-de* 'each own's' in (13a), but not in (13b).

In short, based on these two differences noted above—the semantic licensing of duration adverbs by V$_2$, and possible antecedents for an anaphoric possessor contained in the theme object of V$_2$, Y. Li argues that V-V and V-*de* constructions have different syntactic structures. He maintains that, while V-*de* resultatives have a biclausal structure, V-V resultative compounds enter the syntax as single verbs—that is, they are generated in the lexicon.

Y. Li's analysis, however, faces challenges. First, as mentioned in footnote 5, the test suggested by Y. Li on the different binding properties of V-V and V-*de* resultatives, which is crucial for his analysis, requires that the second verb (V$_2$) in the resultative V-V constructions be associated with two arguments, an external argument

---

Mandarin demonstrates complex properties. For the current concern, briefly speaking, one property of the *BA* construction is that the morpheme *BA* can provide a slot for an extra argument in the post-*BA* position in the surface string. In the two examples in (13), the causee external argument of V$_2$, which is 'extra' when V$_2$ also carries a theme object, is introduced by *BA*, and it appears in the post-*BA* position.

[3]In contrast to Y. Li's analysis, Zhang (2007) offers a pure syntactic analysis of the binding contrast in (13). Zhang proposes that if a V-V resultative is derived by head movement, an equidistance effect occurs, and thus the two binding possibilities are both available.

and a theme object. However, this is unusual for resultative V-V constructions, as normally V_2 in resultative V-V constructions is an unaccusative, and is associated with just one argument. Y. Li resorts to the *BA* construction to construct these special testing examples. In my judgment, however, the example in (13a) is very marginal, if it is acceptable at all.

Secondly, Y. Li's lexical analysis predicts that V-V resultatives can be modified by adverbs as a whole, but their components cannot be modified independently—that is, V_1 or V_2 cannot be targeted by adverbial modification separately. In Chap. 3, I will focus on the adverbial modification properties of resultative V-V compounds, and show that adverbs actually can modify the two component verbal morphemes of resultative V-V compounds separately. This property is difficult to explain under Y. Li's lexical-generation analysis.

In the next section, I provide a syntactic-generation analysis for the two types of V-V compounds in Mandarin, resultative and parallel V-V compounds, and demonstrate that the two-domain hypothesis provides a natural explanation for their contrasting properties.

2.5   Generation of Resultative and Parallel V-V Compounds in Mandarin

In this section, I first introduce parallel V-V compounds, and then illustrate the contrasting properties of resultative and parallel V-V compounds (Sect. 2.5.1).[4] Then I provide my analysis of the generation of these two types of compounds (Sect. 2.5.2). Adopting the two-domain hypothesis, I argue that, for parallel V-V compounds, the two roots combine first to form a root complex, and this root complex then merge with the verbalizing head (little *v*), as in (14a). On the other hand, for resultative V-V compounds, each of the two roots first merges with their own verbalizing head little *v* to form two *v*Ps, and then these two *v*Ps combine to form the V-V compound, as illustrated in (14b).

(14) a. Formation of parallel V-V compounds   b. Formation of resultative V-V compounds

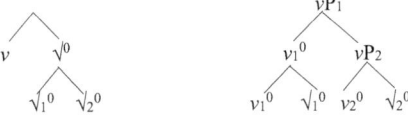

---

[4]In this section, I will provide a number of examples of Mandarin parallel V-V compounds. Note that, for al these examples, judgments are mine as a native Mandarin speaker, unless otherwise indicated.

2.5.1   *Resultative Versus Parallel V-V Compounds*

2.5.1.1   **Parallel V-V Compounds**

Like resultative V-V compounds, parallel V-V compounds are widely used in Mandarin. But unlike resultative V-V compounds, in which the two verbal morphemes combine to express a 'cause-result' meaning, the defining character-istic of parallel V-V compounds is that they are composed of two verbal morphemes that have the same or similar meaning, or the two component morphemes denote the same type of predicative notions. "[T]he two verbs that constitute a parallel verb compound either are synonymous or signal the same type of predicative notions" (Li & Thompson, 1981, p. 30). It is assumed that semantically these two morphemes contribute to the meaning of the whole compound equally (Fabb, 1998). To further demonstrate this type of compound, we consider some examples. First, we consider *xuan-ze* 'to choose'. In this compound, the two component morphemes *xuan* and *ze* have the same meaning of 'to select, to choose', and the compound also means 'to select'. More examples in which the two morphemes have the same or similar meanings are given in (15).

(15) | *pronunciation* | *character* | *literal gloss* | *meaning* |
|---|---|---|---|
| qing-zhu | 庆-祝 | celebrate-celebrate | 'to celebrate' |
| bi-jiao | 比-较 | compare-compare | 'to compare' |
| zhan-dou | 战-斗 | fight-fight, contest with | 'to fight' |
| da-ji | 打-击 | beat-hit | 'to hit' |
| gai-bian | 改-变 | change-become different | 'to change' |
| si-nian | 思-念 | miss-miss, think about | 'to miss' |
| bang-zhu | 帮-助 | help-help, assist | 'to help' |
| guan-cha | 观-察 | watch-watch, check | 'to watch, to observe' |
| ben-pao | 奔-跑 | run fast-run | 'to run (fast)' |
| chuan-di | 传-递 | pass, transmit-deliver | 'to transmit' |

In some parallel V-V compounds, the two components do not have the same or similar meaning, rather they denote the same type of predicative notions. For example, in the parallel compound *zhi-hui* 'to command', the two component morphemes have different literal meanings: *zhi* means 'to point' (e.g., with one's hand or finger), and *hui* means 'to wave, to brandish' (e.g., one's hands). However, as *zhi* and *hui* can both denote the physical movement of one's hands (or arms) when one is commanding, as, for example, a conductor leading a symphony orchestra, or a general commanding a charge on a battlefield, these two morphemes combine to form the compound *zhi-hui* 'to command', a member of the other type of parallel compounds. More examples of this type of parallel V-V compound are given in (16).

(16) | *pronunciation* | *character* | *literal gloss* | *meaning* |
| --- | --- | --- | --- |
| ji-jiao | 计-较 | calculate-compare | 'to haggle over' |
| xiao-mie | 消-灭 | disappear-extinguish | 'to eliminate, to abolish' |
| bao-wei | 包-围 | wrap-surround | 'to surround' |
| zhe-teng | 折-腾 | fold-jump | 'to toss about' |
| pi-ping | 批-评 | criticize-comment | 'to criticize' |
| guan-li | 管-理 | supervise-sort out | 'to administrate' |
| zhi-chi | 支-持 | prop-hold | 'to support' |
| feng-suo | 封-锁 | seal-lock | 'to block' |

Another feature of parallel V-V compounds is that they can be formed from either free or bound morphemes. The parallel V-V compound *gai-bian* 'to change', for example, is formed from two free morphemes, as both the morphemes *gai* 'to change, to alter' and *bian* 'to change, to become different' can be used independently, as in (17).

(17) a. wo **gai**　zhuyi-le.
　　　 I　change idea-ASP
　　　 'I changed my idea.'

　　 b. tade taidu　**bian**-le.
　　　 his　attitude change-ASP
　　　 'His attitude changed.'

On the other hand, the parallel V-V compound *guan-cha* 'to observe' is formed by two bound morphemes. In old Mandarin, both *guan* and *cha* were free verbal morphemes, with *guan* meaning 'to watch', and *cha* meaning 'to observe, to sense'. In modern Chinese, the morphemes *guan* and *cha* can no longer function as independent verbs on their own. Instead, modern Mandarin uses the compound *guan-cha*, rather than the single morpheme of *guan* or *cha*, to mean 'to observe'. It should be noted, however, that the two verbal morphemes of *guan* and *cha*, typical of most parallel V-V compounds, have independent distributions outside the compound *guan-cha*; that is, each of them can combine with other verbal morphemes to form new compounds. The morpheme *guan* can form, for example, *guan-kan* 'to see, to watch', *guan-shang* 'to watch and appreciate', and *guan-ce* 'to watch and measure'. Likewise, the morpheme *cha* can appear in such parallel V-V compounds as *jian-cha* 'to inspect', *he-cha* 'to check', and *diao-cha* 'to investigate'. These properties of *guan-cha* 'to observe' are typical of the majority of parallel V-V compounds.

2.5.1.2　Contrasting Properties of Resultative and Parallel V-V Compounds

While resultative V-V compounds and parallel V-V compounds are superficially similar, they demonstrate systematically different properties, as summarized in (18).

(18) Contrasting properties of resultative and parallel V-V compounds

Properties	Resultative V-V compounds	Parallel V-V compounds
Permit idiosyncratic semantics	No	Yes
Nominal use	No	Yes
Permit bound morphemes	No	Yes
Fully productive	Yes	No
Partial modification	Yes	No

In the next section, I will present these contrasting properties of the two types of V-V compounds, and show that the two-domain hypothesis can provide a natural explanation of these contrasting properties.

2.5.2   An Analysis Under the Two-Domain Hypothesis

2.5.2.1   Semantics: Compositionality Versus Idiosyncrasy

A first contrasting property of the two types of V-V compounds is that, while the meanings of resultative V-V compounds are composed from the literal meanings of the two components, parallel V-V compounds generally demonstrate semantic idiosyncrasy in that the compound meaning is not (always) exactly composed from the literal meanings of the two components. We consider resultative compounds first, taking *kan-dao* 'cut-fall' as an example. In Mandarin, the verbal morpheme *kan* means 'to cut', and *dao* means 'to fall'. The compound *kan-dao* means 'to cut (something) so that it falls'. It is obvious that the meaning of the compound is a transparent combination of the literal meanings of its two components. Note that this transparency is a consistent property of resultative V-V compounds in Mandarin.

The semantics of parallel V-V compounds, in contrast, demonstrates a degree of idiosyncratic variation from the literal meanings of the two components. For most parallel compounds, while the meaning of the compound is based on the meaning of the two components, the compound meaning is nonetheless not equivalent to the combination of the literal meanings of its components. Instead, in most cases, these compounds tend to express an abstract figurative meaning associated with the literal meaning of the two components. Consider the parallel V-V compound *zhe-mo*. The morpheme *zhe* means 'to fold, to bend', and *mo* means 'to rub, to grind', as illustrated in (19a-b). The compound *zhe-mo*, however, means 'to torture' (20).

(19) a. haizimen zhengzai **zhe** zhi   wan-er.
         children PROG   fold paper for.fun
         'The children are folding paper for fun.'

     b. ta zhengzai **mo** yi-ba   dao.
        he PROG   rub   one-CL knife
        'He is rubbing a knife (to sharpen it).'

(20) a. tamen cong routishang **zhe-mo**   John.
       they   from body   bend-rub John
       'They tortured John physically.'

     b. tamen tongguo bu rang   Bill jian tade er-zi lai **zhe-mo**   ta.
        they   by   not allow Bill*i* see his*i* son to bend-rub him*i*
        'They tortured Bill*i* by not allowing him*i* to see his*i* son.'

Moreover, in some parallel V-V compounds, the literal meanings of the two components are indeed not available. For example, (20a) does not mean that they tortured John by physically bending his body and rubbing his body (against some rough surface). On the other hand, imagine the situation that John is bending an iron bar and also rubbing it (against some rough surface) in trying to get it into a particular shape. For this situation, Mandarin speakers cannot use the compound *zhe-mo*, as shown in (21).

(21) *John zhengzai **zhe-mo**   na-gen tiebang.
     John PROG   bend-rub that-CL iron.bar
     Intended meaning: 'John is bending and rubbing that iron bar.'

This discrepancy of the semantics of the parallel compounds from the semantics of their components can also be demonstrated by the glosses of the examples in (16) above. I give some more examples in (22).

(22)

pronunciation	*character*	*literal gloss*	*meaning*
shang-liang	商-量	consult-measure	'to discuss, to talk over'
jiao-liu	交-流	intersect-flow	'to communicate'
xi-guan	习-惯	practice-get.used.to	'to get used to'
xiang-nian	想-念	think about-miss	'to miss'
lian-xi	联-系	connect-tie	'to contact'

It should be noted that the semantic discrepancy between parallel V-V compounds and their components can vary. While some parallel compounds demonstrate a higher degree of semantic transparency, others demonstrate a lower degree. We show this by comparing the two parallel compounds *shang-hai* 'to hurt' and *dao-gu* 'to fiddle with'. In *shang-hai* 'to hurt', the component *shang* means 'to injure', and *hai* means 'to impair, to damage'. It is easy to see that the meaning of the compound *shang-hai* 'to hurt' is quite close to the meaning of its components—demonstrating a higher degree of semantic transparency. In (23) are some more examples of this group (also see examples in (15) above).

(23)

pronunciation	*character*	*literal gloss*	*meaning*
gong-ji	攻-击	attack-hit	'to attack'
xuan-ze	选-择	choose-select	'to choose'
yao-huang	搖-晃	rock-sway	'to shake'
xia-jiang	下-降	come down-descend	'to drop'
peng-zhuang	碰-撞	bump into-collide	'to collide'
yun-shu	运-输	transport-convey	'to transport'

The parallel V-V compound *dao-gu* 'to fiddle with', on the other hand, illustrates the other extreme. The morpheme *dao* means 'to pound, to smash', and *gu* means 'to bulge, to pout'. The meaning of the compound *dao-gu* 'to fiddle with', obviously, is quite different from the meanings of its components. This example thus represents another group of parallel V-V compounds that demonstrate a low degree of transparency, or in other words, a high degree of semantic deviation from the meaning of their components. More examples are provided in (24).

(24) | *pronunciation* | *character* | *literal gloss* | *meaning* |
|---|---|---|---|
| zheng-zha | 挣-扎 | prop-entwine | 'to struggle' |
| zhe-teng | 折-腾 | bend-soar | 'to be restless and cause trouble' |
| hui-huo | 挥-霍 | wield-dispel | 'to squander' |
| da-ban | 打-扮 | hit-pretend | 'to dress up' |
| liu-fang | 流-放 | flow-release | 'to exile' |

Finally, to further demonstrate this contrast between resultative and parallel V-V compounds, let us consider the situation in which both resultative and parallel V-V compounds are formed by the same set of component verbal morphemes. We consider the two verbal morphemes *zhe* 'to fold, to bend' and *mo* 'to rub, to grind' again. In addition to the compound *zhe-mo*, the two verbal morphemes *zhe* and *mo* can combine with other verbal morphemes to form different parallel V-V compounds. For example, *zhe* can combine with the morpheme *teng* 'to jump high, to soar' to form the parallel compound *zhe-teng*, meaning 'to be restless and cause trouble'; *mo* can combine with the morpheme *zhuo* 'to carve', to form the parallel compound *zhuo-mo*, meaning 'to contemplate, to think carefully and thoroughly'. Note that all these parallel V-V compounds demonstrate idiosyncratic deviation from the literal meanings of their components.

On the other hand, *zhe* and *mo* can also combine with other verb morphemes to form resultative V-V compounds. For example, *zhe* can combine with the verb morpheme *duan* 'break' to form *zhe-duan*, meaning 'to bend something so that it breaks' (25a); *mo* can combine with *lan* 'to be messy, to be worn out' to form the resultative compound *mo-lan*, meaning 'to be rubbed until worn out' (25b). Note that when the morphemes *zhe* and *mo* form a resultative V-V compound, the meaning of the compound is always the combination of their literal meanings.

(25) a. John **zhe-duan**-le   na-gen mu   bang.
         John bend-break-ASP that-CL wood stick
         'John bent and broke that wood stick.'

     b. John de   kujiao   **mo-lan**-le.
         John DE (possessive) jeans.cuff rub-be.messy-ASP
         'The cuffs of John's jeans got worn out by rubbing (against the road).'

Adopting the two-domain hypothesis, I propose that the semantic compositionality versus idiosyncrasy of resultative and parallel V-V compounds is due to the fact that they are formed in different syntactic domains. I argue that parallel V-V compounds are generated in the inner (root) domain, where two acategorical roots merge first, and then this root complex merges with the functional categorizing head *v*. This analysis accounts for the semantic idiosyncrasy of parallel V-V compounds, as one property associated with the inner domain is semantic idiosyncrasy. On the other hand, I propose that resultative V-V compounds are formed in the outer domain: that is, they are the combination of two categorized verbs v_1P and v_2P. Specifically, after each of the roots merges with a separate v, these two roots are categorized as verbs, and their meanings become frozen. This analysis accounts for why the meanings of resultative V-V compounds are compositional and predictable from the meanings of their component verbs.

According to Marantz (2010), the different semantic properties of complex words formed by adding a morpheme in the inner domain versus the outer domain are the manifestation of a more general mechanism—contextual allosemy. We can further account for the semantic differences between parallel and resultative V-V compounds by appealing to this mechanism. Marantz (2010) argues that the grammar must choose an alloseme of any polysemous element at the point of semantic composition. Specifically, the choice among the possible meanings of a polysemous element is determined by its context—that is, by the elements "that combine (directly) semantically" with this element (p. 10). Marantz also proposes that the locality domain for contextual allosemy is the nearest phase. That is, the elements which are in the same phase as the polysemous element and which combine directly semantically with it will form the context in which the meaning of this polysemous element is determined. Marantz specifically provides the example of the root *novel* to demonstrate this contextual allosemy mechanism. He proposes that the root *novel* can mean either a concrete physical object (e.g., *The novel on my table weights 2 lb*), or an abstract work of art (e.g., *The novel on my table is gripping*). In the context of the verbalizing head *-ize*, it is the latter alloseme of *novel* that is chosen. That is, the verbalizing head selects the abstract work of art meaning, and resists the meaning that involves the physical object alloseme of the root.

Assuming this contextual allosemy hypothesis, I propose that, in Mandarin, many verbal roots, like the nominal root of *novel* in English, are polysemous with (at least) two meanings, a literal (concrete) meaning and a figurative (abstract) meaning. Also given the assumption that the first merged little x forms a phase (Marantz, 2000, 2007), I propose that, in parallel V-V compounds, the context for allosemy of (each of) the two morphemes is the sister root morpheme that has the similar meaning or indicates a similar predicative notion. That is, the two root morphemes constitute each other's allosemy context. I propose that, in this context, it is a figurative meaning that may be chosen, and this is why the meaning of parallel V-V compounds demonstrates semantic idiosyncrasy. In resultative V-V compounds, by contrast, the allosemy context for each verbal root is just the first merged little v. That is to say, unlike parallel V-V compounds, the two roots of resultative V-V compounds appear in two separate allosemy contexts or domains, and these contexts choose the usual literal meaning of the verbal morpheme. This is why the meanings of resultative V-V compounds always reflect the literal meanings of their component verbal morphemes.[5]

---

[5]If the two-domain hypothesis and the contextual allosemy analysis of the semantic difference between Mandarin resultative and parallel V-V compounds is correct, a further question arises: why in the case of parallel V-V compounds is it that the abstract alloseme is chosen, while in the case

Before finishing this section, we consider still another situation, that is, some resultative V-V compounds do seem to have a figurative (non-literal) meaning too, as noted by Zhang (personal communication). For example, the meaning of the resultative V-V compound *da-po* 'hit-break' has a figurative meaning as in *da-po chen-gui* 'break the old rules', in additioin to the usual literal interpretation in many of its uses. I leave this issue for future work.

2.5.2.2   Nominalizations

The second contrast between resultative and parallel V-V compounds is in their (un)availability to be used as nouns. In Mandarin, most (if not all) parallel V-V compounds can also be used as nouns (without morphological or phonological change). I demonstrate this property with the two compounds *fang-wen* 'visit' and *an-pai* 'arrange(ment)' in (26)–(27).

(26) a. *fang-wen* used as a verb 'to visit'
      qunian   zongtong   **fang-wen**-le meiguo.
      last.year president visit-ASP   America
      'The president visited America last year.'

    b. *fang-wen* used as a noun 'visit'
      na   shi yi-ci   chenggongde **fang-wen**.
      that be one-CL successful   visit
      'That was a successful visit.'

In (26a), the parallel compound *fang-wen* 'visit' appears after the subject DP *zongtong* 'president', and is followed by the aspectual marker *le*, and then an object. This is the canonical position for the main verb in a declarative clause in Mandarin, and this example therefore indicates that the compound *fang-wen* 'visit' in this clause is used as a verb. In (26b), in contrast, *fang-wen* 'visit' appears in a position that is typically occupied by nouns. Specifically, *fang-wen* in this clause is preceded and modified by an adjective *chenggongde* 'successful'; also it combines with the quantifier *yi-ci* 'one (time)', which normally combines with NPs; the whole constituent *yici chenggongde fang-wen* 'one successful visit', in which *fang-wen* is the head, occurs after the main verb *shi* 'to be' and functions as its complement. All these factors indicate that, in this clause, the complex word *fang-wen* is used as a noun. Another example, which is based on *an-pai* 'arrange(ment)', is given in (27).

---

of resultative V-V compounds, it is the literal meaning that is chosen? The present study has no answer to this question, and I leave it for future work.

(27) a. *an-pai* as a verb 'to arrange'
  wo **an-pai**-le   yige juhui qinghe   tade shengri.
  I   arrange-ASP one party celebrate his birthday
  'I arranged a party to celebrate his birthday.'

  b. *an-pai* as a noun 'arrangement'
  huiyi   de   chenggong shouxian shi youyu ta zhoumide **an-pai**.
  meeting DE (possessive) success   firstly   be due.to his meticulous arrangement
  'The success of the meeting is firstly due to his meticulous arrangement.'

Resultative V-V compounds, in contrast, can only be used as verbs, and cannot be used as nouns. I demonstrate this by taking the compounds *chi-pang* 'to eat and be fat' and *jiao-xing* 'to call and wake (somebody)' in (28) and (29) as examples. In (28a), the compounds *chi-pang* 'to eat and be fat' occupies the canonical verb position of a Mandarin declarative clause: it follows the DP that functions as the subject, and is followed by the aspectual marker *le*. This indicates that the compound *chi-pang* 'to eat and be fat' is used as a verb. In (28b), however, when we put *chi-pang* 'to eat and be fat' in a canonical NP position (as just described), this sentence is clearly ill-formed.

(28) a. *chi-pang* used as a verb
    John **chi-pang**-le.
    John eat-be.fat-ASP
    'John ate (a lot) and got fat.'

  b. *chi-pang* used as a noun
    *na shi yi-ci   chenggongde **chi-pang**.
    that is one-CL successful   eat-be.fat
    Intended meaning: 'That is a successful (event of) eating a lot and getting fat.'
    [For medical reasons, John needed to eat a lot to get fat, and he did it successfully.]

Below, (29) is a parallel example with the compound *jiao-xing* 'to call and wake (somebody)'. Note that, when this compound appears in another typical NP position—as the head of the subject NP, and combined with a possessive pronoun—the sentence is ungrammatical.

(29) a. *jiao-xing* used as a verb
    ta **jiao-xing**-le   Bill.
    he call-wake-ASP Bill
    'He woke Bill by calling him.'

  b. *jiao-xing* used as a noun
    *tade **jiao-xing** (Bill) jinu-le   Bill.
    his   call-wake Bill   irritate-ASP Bill
    Intended meaning: 'He irritated Bill$_i$ by calling and waking him$_i$ up.'

With regard to the unavailability of the nominal use for resultative V-V compounds, we still need to consider two issues: the counterexamples to this generalization, and an account of the restriction on nominalizing resultative V-V compounds. I address these two issues next.

First, it seems that some of the V-V resultative compounds can be used as nouns. We consider the compound *niu-shang* 'sprain' (literal: to twist-be injured). *Niu-shang* is a resultative V-V compound, meaning 'to twist and as a result get injured', as shown in (30a). However, this compound can also be used as a noun, meaning 'an injury caused by a twist', as illustrated in (30b). Other similar examples include *shao-shang* 'to burn-be injured', which can be used as a verb meaning 'to burn and (as a result) to cause an injury', or it can be used as a noun, meaning 'an injury from being burnt'.

(30) a. *niu-shang* used as a resultative V-V compound

  ta **niu-shang**-le   houbei.
  he twist-get.injured-ASP back
  'He sprained his back.'

 b. *niu-shang* used as a noun

  tade houbei you yi-chu **niu-shang**.
  his back there.be one-CL sprain
  'He got a sprain in his back.'

Compounds like *niu-shang* constitute counterexamples to my analysis. However, if we examine the other resultative compounds formed by the two morphemes of *niu* 'to twist' and *shang* 'to injure/injury', we can make the following observations. First, the morpheme *niu* 'to twist' can form a variety of resultative V-V compounds, some of which are listed in (31). Notably, none of these compounds can be used as a noun.

(31)

pronunciation	*character*	*literal gloss*	*meaning*
niu-duan	扭-断	twist-break	'to break by twisting'
niu-wan	扭-弯	twist-curve	'to curve by twisting'
niu-jin	扭-紧	twist-be tight	'to tighten by twisting'
niu-gan	扭-干	twist-dry	'to dry by twisting (a towel)'

Among the compounds that the morpheme *shang* 'to injure/injury' can form, some of them, as the ones listed in (32), can be used as nouns (in addition to being used as verbs); others, notably, can only be used as verbs, but not nouns, such as the ones listed in (33).

(32) Compounds allowing noun use

pronunciation	*character*	*literal gloss*	*meaning*
ca-shang	擦-伤	scratch-hurt	verb: 'to scratch and get injured'
			noun: 'bruise, scratch'
la-shang	拉-伤	pull-hurt	verb: 'to pull and get injured'
			noun: 'strain'
tang-shang	烫-伤	heat-hurt	verb: 'to heat and get injured'
			noun: 'empyrosis'

(33) Compounds disallowing noun use

pronunciation	character	literal gloss	meaning
kan-shang	砍-伤	cut-hurt	'to cut and cause injury'
tong-shang	捅-伤	stab-hurt	'to stab and cause injury'
da-shang	打-伤	beat-hurt	'to beat and cause injury'
zha-shang	炸-伤	explode-hurt	'to explode and cause injury'

In Mandarin the morpheme *shang* (?) 'to injure/injury' can be used as either a verb, as demonstrated in (34a), or a noun 'injury, wound', as in (34b).

(34) a. zhe-jian-shi **shang**-le tade xin.
   this-CL-thing hurt-ASP his heart
   'This thing made him feel bruised of heart.'

   b. tade **shang** hen zhong.
   his wound very serious
   'His wound is very bad.'

Based on these observations—in particular, based on the property of *shang* that it can be a noun or a verb—I argue that, for the 'V+ *shang*' compounds that have both nominal and verbal uses (the examples in (30b) and (32)), they actually have different internal structures, while having the same morphological form. Specifically, while the verbal 'V+ *shang*' forms are V-V compounds, i.e. verbalized v-v, nominal 'V+ *shang*' forms are actually V–N compounds, in which the nominal component *shang* 'injury' functions as the head of the compound. Given this analysis, and also considering that the number of the counterexamples like *niu-shang* 'twist-be injured' is comparatively small, I will maintain the observation that resultative V-V compounds cannot be used as nouns.

We now consider the second issue, that is, what accounts for the impossibility of nominalizing resultative V-V compounds in Mandarin. In some languages, *v*Ps can be nominalized (in certain cases). For example, Harley (2005) argues that the expression in English *mixing of drugs and alcohol* as in *Belushi's foolish mixing of drugs and alcohol was the cause of his death* is a nominalization of *v*P. In this chapter, I have argued that V_1 and V_2 in resultative V-V compounds, unlike the two verbal roots in parallel V-V compounds, are each associated with a different *v*P. However, it seems that the nominalization of resultative V-V compounds is never possible in Mandarin. I provide two more examples in (35), which again indicate that the *v*Ps associated with resultative V-V compounds cannot be nominalized. As argued above, this is a property of all resultative V-V compounds, to the best of my knowledge.

(35) a. *John de   **kan-dao** naxie shu jinu-le   cun-min.
   John DE (possessive) cut-fall those tree anger-ASP villager
   Intended meaning: 'John's cutting down of those trees angered the villagers.'

   b. *naxie shu de   **kan-dao** qingchu-le   zuihoude zhangai.
   those tree DE (possessive) cut-fall remove-ASP last   obstacle
   Intended meaning: 'The cutting down of those trees removed the last obstacle.'

Returning to our analysis of the contrast in the possibility of nominalizing the two types of V-V compounds, I argue that this contrast can find a straightforward account under the two-domain hypothesis. As I have proposed, the central syntactic difference between resultative and parallel V-V compounds is that the former are the combination of two categorized verbs (*v*Ps), while the latter involve the initial merge of two acategorical roots, followed by the merge of this root complex with a categorizing functional head (little *x*). For resultative V-V compounds, this generation process entails that they must function as verbs, as they are based on two categorized verbs, and the merge operation cannot change this syntactic property.

The situation of parallel V-V compounds is more variable, in that the selection relation between the roots needs not specify the categorizing head that their root-complex might merge with. Within a DM framework, it has been proposed that roots can be further classified in terms of basic ontological types such as 'individual', 'state', and 'event' (cf. Harley, 2005; Levinson, 2007, 2010; Marantz, 2013). These authors also postulate that the relation between the lexical roots and the categorizing heads that they merge with is a modifying relation. Specifically, the three categorizing heads *v*, *n*, and *a* introduce events, entities, and states, respectively, and the roots belonging to relevant semantic types merge with corresponding heads as event modifiers, entity modifiers, and state modifiers. Marantz (2010) points out that another manifestation of the semantic idiosyncrasy of the root is that certain lexical roots might be ambiguous between entity versus event modifiers. For example, the root *jump* in English can be either an entity modifier when used in *a jump*, or an event modifier when used in *to jump*. I propose that the abstract root allosemes of Mandarin parallel V-V compounds possess a similar property. That is, they can be either event modifiers, merging with little *v* and generating parallel V-V compounds, or entity modifiers, merging with little *n* and generating compound nouns. As the categorizing heads in Mandarin are morphologically null (cf. Zhang, 2007), we observe the phenomenon that parallel V-V compounds can function as either verbs or nouns. That is, they can be nominalized, unlike resultative V-V compounds.

2.5.2.3 Free Versus Bound Component Morphemes

Resultative and parallel V-V compounds contrast in yet another respect: while resultative compounds are always formed by free morphemes, parallel V-V compounds tend to be formed with bound morphemes. We consider resultative compounds first, taking *kan-dao* 'cut-fall' as an example again (36a). As demonstrated in (36b) and (36c), the two morphemes *kan* 'to cut' and *dao* 'to fall' are both free morphemes, and can function as main verbs independently.

(36) a. John **kan-dao**-le yi-ke shu.
      John cut-fall-ASP a-CL tree
      'John cut down a tree.'

    b. John zhengzai yong dao **kan** shuzhi.
      John PROG   with knife cut branch
      'John is cutting the branches with a knife.'

    c. na-ke   shu **dao**-le.
      that-CL tree fall-ASP
      'That tree fell.'

Parallel V-V compounds, on the other hand, tend to be formed with bound morphemes, as briefly introduced in Sect. 2.5.1.1. Regarding the free versus bound morphemes in parallel V-V compounds, several patterns can be observed. In the first place, a few parallel V-V compounds are formed by two free morphemes, such as *ti-ba* 'to promote'. In this compound, both *ti* 'to carry, to lift upward' and *ba* 'to pull upward' are free morphemes and can be used independently as main verbs. Similar examples include *yao-huang* 'to shake', *gai-bian* 'to change', and *chuan-di* 'to transmit'.

In the second pattern, some parallel compounds are formed with one bound morpheme and one free morpheme. In the parallel compound *xue-xi*, for example, the first morpheme *xue* 'to study' is a free morpheme; the second morpheme *xi*, however, is a bound morpheme, which cannot function as an independent predicate, but can combine with other morphemes to form various compounds, such as *yan-xi* 'to maneuver' and *lian-xi* 'to practise'. Similarly, in the compound *qi-qiu*, the second morpheme *qiu* 'to ask for (by begging)' is a free morpheme; the first morpheme *qi* 'to beg, to plead', however, is a bound morpheme, which also occurs in *qi-tao* 'to go begging'.

Thirdly, for a large proportion of parallel compounds, both components are bound morphemes. Compounds like *jian-du* 'to monitor, to supervise', *guan-cha* 'to observe', and *yan-jiu* 'to research' all belong to this group. But note that, for this group of compounds, their component morphemes have their own literal meanings, and have independent distributions; that is, they can combine with various morphemes to form different compounds. We take *jian-du* 'to monitor' as an example. The morpheme *jian* 'to monitor' can form compounds like *jian-guan* 'to supervise', and *jian-shi* 'to keep watch on'; the morpheme *du* 'to supervise' can form the compounds *du-cha* 'to inspect', and *du-cu* 'to urge'.

Finally, for a small number of parallel compounds, the two component morphemes in isolation do not carry distinct meanings in Mandarin (i.e. modern Chinese), and must combine with each other to form a compound to convey a distinct meaning. Compounds in this group include *pai-huai* 'to wander', *you-yu* 'to hesitate', and *pao-xiao* 'to roar'.

I argue that this contrast regarding free versus bound component morphemes constitutes another piece of evidence for the analysis that resultative compounds are formed from two verbs, while parallel V-V compounds are based on the combination of two acategorical roots. In the DM framework, besides being free or bound, morphemes are also divided into lexical root morphemes and functional morphemes.

Lexical morphemes are 'content' morphemes bearing lexical meanings, while functional morphemes are the realization (spell-out) of functional heads. Within the DM framework, one basic assumption is that the merge of lexical root morphemes always occurs in the inner domain. I demonstrate this with the example of English word *gloriousness* provided in Marantz (2000). According to Marantz, *gloriousness* is formed as illustrated in (37). First, the lexical root morpheme vGLORY merges with the phonologically null little *n* to form the noun *glory*; the noun *glory* then merges with little *a*, which is realized by the morpheme *-ous*, to form the adjective *glorious*; finally, the adjective *glorious* merges with another little *n* head, which is spelled out as *-ness*, and we get the complex noun *gloriousness*. In this example, the morpheme *GLORY* is a lexical root morpheme, which provides the basic meaning of the complex word, while the morphemes *ous* and *ness* are functional morphemes. Also, while the merges of the functional morphemes of *ous* and *ness* occur in the outer domain, above the first merged functional head, the lexical morpheme *GLORY* merges below the first merged little *n* head, i.e. in the inner domain.

(37)

Note that in parallel V-V compounds in Mandarin, the two component morphemes are lexical morphemes providing meaning for the compounds (Li & Thompson, 1981; Pirani, 2008). This property entails that the merge of these compounds occurs in the inner domain. Alaso, as just mentioned, the component morphemes in most parallel V-V compounds are bound morphemes. This indicates that these morphemes themselves cannot combine directly with the first merged fincional head. Rather, before merging with a functional head, these bound lexical morphemes must first merge with another lexical morpheme. That is to say, the combination of the two component morphemes of parallel V-V compounds occurs in the inner domain. In contrast, for resultative V-V compounds, the component morphemes are free morphenes, which means that each of the two components can combine with the little *v* head to form two *v*Ps, and then the two *v*Ps combine to form a resultative V-V compound.

2.5.2.4   Productivity Versus Semi-productivity

Still another contrasting property of resultative and parallel V-V compounds is that, while the former is productive, the latter is only semi-productive at most, demonstrating root-conditioned idiosyncrasy. I assume that this contrast provides another argument for the two-domain formation analysis of these two types of compounds.

The productivity of resultative V-V compounds has been noted in the literature. Shi (2002), for example, notes that in Mandarin any verb-result collocation that makes sense is possible. Shi takes the verb *chi* 'to eat' to demonstrate this point, and remarks that "theoretically, any state that can be caused by the action of eating can be used as a resultative with the verb *chi* 'eat'" (p. 32). Shi claims that with the support of proper context, all the cases in (38) are good.

(38)	*pronunciation*	*character*	*literal gloss*	*meaning*
	chi-bao	吃-饱	eat-be.full	to eat and as a result to get full
	chi-ni	吃-腻	eat-be.bored	to eat and as a result to get bored
	chi-bing	吃-病	eat-be.sick	to eat and as a result to get sick
	chi-pang	吃-胖	eat-be.fat	to eat and as a result to get fat
	chi-qiong	吃-穷	eat-be.poor	to eat and as a result to get poor
	chi-yun	吃-晕	eat-be.dizzy	to eat and as a result to get dizzy
	chi-shou	吃-瘦	eat-be.thin	to eat and as a result to get thin
	chi-lei	吃-累	eat-be.tired	to eat and as a result to get tired
	chi-tu	吃-吐	eat-vomit	to eat and as a result to vomit

Parallel V-V compounds, in contrast, demonstrate considerable idiosyncrasy and are only semi-productive at most. For one thing, unlike resultative V-V compounds, parallel V-V compounds are usually listed in dictionaries, and it is unusual to create new parallel V-V compounds in Mandarin. Moreover, there are obvious gaps and idiosyncrasies in the process of combining two verbal morphemes with similar meanings to designate the single event. To demonstrate this, consider the following example. In Mandarin, the morphemes *nian, gan, qu, zhui, zhu* all have the core meaning of 'to chase, to drive away'. However, in forming parallel compounds, only four combinations, namely *zhui-zhu, zhui-gan, qu-zhu, qu-gan*, are attested to convey the meaning 'to chase away'. Other combinations, such as *gan-nian, qu-nian, zhui-qu,* or *zhui-nian*, are not attested. I assume that these examples demonstrate the semi-productivity of Mandarin parallel V-V compounds.

In my analysis, the contrast in productivity of these two types of V-V compounds follows from their different structures. As posited in the two-domain hypothesis, words generation involving the combination of elements in the inner (root) domain demonstrates root-conditioned idiosyncrasy, while words generation involving the addition of an element in the outer domain demonstrates productivity. I propose that the relative lack of productivity that parallel V-V compounds demonstrate is another manifestation of the idiosyncrasy of the root domain, like the semantic idiosyncrasy that they also demonstrate.

2.5.2.5 Adverbial Modification

The final contrasting property I will discuss is the difference in adverbial modification properties between the two types of V-V compounds. For parallel V-V compounds, adverbs can only modify the compound as a whole unit, that is, the two verbal components cannot be modified separately. For resultative V-V compounds, however, the two verbal components can be modified separately. I argue that this difference also follows from the different structures of the two types of compounds.

We consider the parallel V-V compounds first, taking *xue-xi* 'to learn' as an example. In the compound *xue-xi* 'to learn', the morpheme *xue* means 'to learn, to study', and *xi* means 'to practise'. The meaning of the compound *xue-xi*, however, is 'to study', but not 'to learn and to practise'. As shown in (39), the adverb *nu-li* 'hard' modifies the whole parallel V-V compound, but never the constituent of *xue* or *xi* alone.

(39) John nuli   **xue-xi**   yingyu.
　　　 John with.effort study-practise English
　　 √ 'John is studying English hard.'
　　 * 'John studies English hard and he also practises.'
　　 * 'John studies English and (also) makes great effort in practising.'

Resultative compounds, in contrast, demonstrate different and more complex adverbial modification properties. Adverbial modification properties of resultative V-V compounds will be a focus of my analysis in Chap. 3. Here, I will just give examples to show that adverbs can modify 'into' resultative compounds. Below, in (40a), the adverbs *fennude* 'angrily' and *buqingyuande* 'reluctantly' modify just V_1 *tui* 'to push', but not V_2 *kai* 'to be open'. Likewise, in (40b) the adverb *dakoudakoude* 'with big bites' only modifies V_1 *chi* 'to eat', but not V_2 *guang* 'to be gone'.

(40) a. John fennude/buqingyuande **tui**-kai-le   men.
　　　　John angrily /reluctantly   push-open-ASP door
　　　　'John pushed the door open angrily/reluctantly.'

　　　 b. John dakoudakode **chi**-guang-le   wan-li-de   fan.
　　　　　John with.big.bites eat-be.gone-ASP in.the.bowl   food
　　　　　'John ate up the food in the bowl with big bites.'

When adverbs such as *henkuai* 'very soon' modify resultative compounds, the sentences have two readings, as exemplified in (41). Note that, for the second reading of (41), the adverb *henkuai* 'very soon' modifies V_2 *dao* 'fall', but not V_1 *cut* 'to cut'. The examples in (40) and (41) thus demonstrate another contrast with parallel compounds.

(41) John henkuai kan-**dao**-le na-ke   shu.
　　　 John very.soon cut-fall-ASP that-CL tree
　　　 i. '(I told John to cut down that tree, and) he did so immediately.'
　　　 ii. 'John cut that tree and in no time the tree fell.'

This contrast between resultative and parallel V-V compounds, I argue, stems from their formation in different domains. I have proposed that resultative and parallel V-V compounds have different syntactic structures: a resultative compound contains two *v*Ps, while a parallel compound has only one *v*P. It has been generally agreed in the literature that (certain) adverbs target events (Tenny & Pustejovsky, 2000), which are syntactically realized as *v*P (cf. Harley 1995; Marantz, 2013; Pylkkänen, 2008). If we adopt these premises, the contrasting adverbial modification property receives a straightforward account. In resultative V-V compounds, the two verb roots are dominated by separate *v*Ps, and therefore they can each be modified by adverbs. For parallel compounds, there is only one *v*P, and its two component roots do not correspond to separate events—that is why they cannot be targeted by event-modifying adverbs separately.

2.6 Conclusion

In this chapter, I investigated the locus of generation for resultative V-V compounds in Mandarin by comparing them with another type of V-V compounds, parallel V-V compounds. I have demonstrated that these two types of V-V compounds, while superficially similar in that both are composed with two verbal morphemes, possess systematically different properties, including compositional versus idiosyncratic meanings, potential for nominalization, free versus bound component morphemes, productivity versus semi-productivity, and different adverbial modification properties. I then show that these contrasting properties can find a natural account under the inner versus outer domain hypothesis for the composition of complex words. Based on these observations, I have proposed that parallel V-V compounds are formed within the root domain—in that the two acategorical roots ($v_1 + v_2$) combine first, and then merge with the functional head little *v*—while resultative V-V compounds are formed by combining two categorized verbs.

Having examined the generation of resultative V-V compounds, in the next chapter, I will consider the syntactic structure of these constructions. Based on their adverbial modification properties, I will propose an analysis of the syntactic structures of resultative V-V constructions in Mandarin.

References

Anagnostopoulou, E., & Samioti, Y. (2013). Allosemy, idioms, and their domains. In R. Folli, C. Sevdali, & R. Truswell (Eds.), *Syntax and its limits* (pp. 218–250). Oxford: Oxford University Press.

Anagnostopoulou, E., & Samioti, Y. (2014). Domains within words and their meanings: A case study. In A. Alexiadou, H. Borer, & F. Schäfer (Eds.), *The syntax of roots and the roots of syntax* (pp. 81–111). Oxford: Oxford University Press.

Anderson, R. (1982). Where's morphology? *Linguistic Inquiry, 13,* 571–612.

Arad, M. (2003). Locality constraints on the interpretation of roots: The case of Hebrew denominal verbs. *Natural Language & Linguistic Theory, 21,* 737–778.

Aronoff, M. (1976). *Word formation in generative grammar*. Cambridge, MA: MIT Press.

Basilico, D. (2008). Particle verbs and benefactive double objects in English: High and low attachment. *Natural Language & Linguistic Theory, 26,* 731–773.

Borer, H. (2005). *Structuring sense, vol. 1: In name only*. Oxford: Oxford University Press.

Bresnan, J., & Mchombo, S. (1995). The lexical integrity principle: Evidence from Bantu. *Natural Language and Linguistic Theory, 13*(2), 181–254.

Bruening, B. (2014). Word formation is syntactic: Adjectival passives in English. *Natural Language & Linguistic Theory, 32,* 363–422.

Chang, J. (2003). Event structure and argument linking in Chinese. *Language and Linguistics, 4*(2), 317–351.

Chang, J. (2007). Linking semantics and syntax in Mandarin serial verbs: A role and reference grammar account. *Language and Linguistics, 8*(1), 235–266.

Cheng, L., & Huang, C.-T. (1994). On the argument structure of resultative compounds. In Y. Chen, J. Ovid, & L. Tzeng (Eds.), *In honour of William S.-Y. Wang: Interdisciplinary studies in language and language change* (pp. 187–221). Taiwan: Pyramid.

Chomsky, N. (1970). Remarks on nominalization. In R. Jacobs & P. Rosenbaum (Eds.), *Readings in English transformational grammar* (pp. 184–221). Waltham, MA: Blaisdell.

Di Sciullo, A., & Williams, E. (1987). *On the definition of word.* Cambridge, MA: MIT Press.

Dubinsky, S., & Simango, S. (1996). Passive and Stative in Chichewa: Evidence for modular distinctions in grammar. *Language, 72,* 749–781.

Embick, D. (2004). On the structure of resultative participles in English. *Linguistic Inquiry, 35,* 355–392.

Embick, D. (2010). *Localism versus globalism in morphology and phonology.* Cambridge, MA: MIT Press.

Fabb, N. (1998). Compounding. In A. Spencer & A. Zwicky (Eds.), *The handbook of morphology* (pp. 66–83). Oxford: Blackwell.

Fodor, J., & Lepore, E. (1998). The emptiness of the lexicon: Reflections on James Pustejovsky's *The Generative Lexicon. Linguistic Inquiry, 29*(2), 269–288.

Halle, M., & Marantz, A. (1993). Distributed morphology and the pieces of inflection. In K. Hale & S. Keyser (Eds.), *The view from building 20* (pp. 111–176). Cambridge, MA: MIT Press.

Harley, H. (1995). *Subjects, events and licensing.* Doctoral dissertation, Massachusetts Institute of Technology.

Harley, H. (2005). How do verbs get their names? Denominal verbs, manner incorporation, and the ontology of verb roots in English. In N. Erteschik-Shir & T. Rapoport (Eds.), *The syntax of aspect. Deriving thematic and aspectual interpretation* (pp. 42–64). Oxford: Oxford University Press.

Huang, C.-T. (1992). Complex predicates in control. In R. Larson, U. Lahiri, S. Iatridou, & J. Higginbotham (Eds.), *Control and grammar* (pp. 109–147). Dordrecht: Kluwer.

Huang, C.-T. (2006). Resultatives and unaccusatives: A parametric view. *Bulletin of the Chinese Linguistic Society of Japan, 253,* 1–43.

Lapointe, S. (1980). *The theory of grammatical agreement.* Doctoral dissertation, University of Massachusetts at Amherst.

Levinson, L. (2007). *The roots of verbs.* Doctoral dissertation, New York University.

Levinson, L. (2010). Arguments for pseudo-resultative predicates. *Natural Language & Linguistic Theory, 28*(1), 135–182.

Li, C. (2013). Mandarin resultative verb compounds: Simple syntax and complex thematic relations. *Language Sciences, 37,* 99–121.

Li, C. (2008). On the headedness of Mandarin resultative verb compounds. In *Proceedings of the 20th North American Conference on Chinese Linguistics* (NACCL-20) (pp. 735–750). Columbus, Ohio: The Ohio State University.

Li, C., & Thompson, S. (1981). *Mandarin Chinese: A functional reference grammar.* Berkeley: University of California Press.

Li, Y. (1990). On V-V compounds in Chinese. *Natural Language & Linguistic Theory, 8,* 177–207.

Li, Y. (1993). Structural head and aspectuality. *Language, 69,* 480–504.

Li, Y. (1998). Chinese resultative constructions and the uniformity of theta assignment hypothesis. In J. Packard (Ed.), *New approaches to Chinese word formation* (pp. 285–310). Berlin: Mouton De Gruyter.

Li, Y. (2005). X^0: *A theory of the morphology-syntax interface.* Cambridge, MA: MIT Press.

Lieber, R. (1980). *On the organization of the lexicon.* Doctoral dissertation, Massachusetts Institute of Technology.

Lin, J. (2004). *Event structure and the encoding of arguments: The syntax of the Mandarin and English verb phrase.* Doctoral dissertation, Massachusetts Institute of Technology.

Liu, H. (2004). *Complex predicates in Mandarin Chinese: Three types of Bu-Yu structures.* Doctoral dissertation, University of California.

Marantz, A. (1997). No escape from syntax: Don't try morphological analysis in the privacy of your own lexicon. In A. Dimitriadis & L. Siegel (Eds.), *University of Pennsylvania Working Papers in Linguistics, vol. 4. Proceedings of the 21st Annual Penn Linguistics Colloquium* (pp. 201–225).

Marantz, A. (2000). *Words.* Unpublished ms. Massachusetts Institute of Technology.

Marantz, A. (2010). *Locality domains for contextual allosemy in words.* Handout: New York University.

Marantz, A. (2013). Verbal argument structure: Events and participants. *Lingua, 130,* 152–168.

Marantz, A., et al. (2007). Phases and words. In S. Choe (Ed.), *Phases in the theory of grammar* (pp. 191–222). Seoul: Dong In.

Nishiyama, K. (1998). V-V compounds as serialization. *Journal of East Asian Linguistics, 7,* 175–217.

Pirani, L. (2008). Bound roots in Mandarin Chinese and comparison with European "Semi-Words". In K. Chan & H. Kang (Eds.), *Proceedings of the 20th North American Conference on Chinese Linguistics* (pp. 261–277). Ohio: The Ohio State University.

Pylkkänen, L. (2008). *Introducing arguments.* Cambridge, MA: MIT Press.

Ramchand, G. (2008). *Verb meaning and the Lexicon: A first-phase syntax.* Cambridge: Cambridge University Press.

Shi, Y. (2002). *The establishment of modern Chinese grammar: The formation of the resultative construction and its effects.* Amsterdam: John Benjamins.

Sugimura, M., & Obata, M. (2016). Outer/inner morphology: The dichotomy of Japanese *renyoo* verbs and nouns. In *Proceedings of the Linguistic Society of America* (pp.1–10).

Svenonius, P. (2005). Review of Dehe´ (2001, Benjamins) Particle verbs in English: Syntax, information structure, and intonation. *Linguistische Berichte, 202,* 261–265.

Tenny, C., & Pustejovsky, J. (2000). A history of events in linguistic theory. In C. Tenny & J. Pustejovsky (Eds.), *Events as grammatical objects*: *The converging perspectives of lexical semantics and syntax* (pp. 3–32). Stanford: CSLI Publications.

Travis, L. (2000). Event structure in syntax. In C. Tenny & J. Pustejovsky (Eds.), *Events as grammatical objects*: *The converging perspectives of lexical semantics and syntax* (pp. 145–185). Stanford: CSLI Publications.

Wang, C. (2010). *The microparametric syntax of resultatives in Chinese languages.* Doctoral dissertation, New York University.

Wasow, T. (1977). Transformations and the lexicon. In P. Culicover, T. Wasow, & A. Akmajian (Eds.), *Formal syntax* (pp. 327–360). New York: Academic Press.

Zhang, N. (2001). The structures of depictive and resultative constructions in Chinese. *ZAS Papers in Linguistics, 22,* 191–221.

Zhang, N. (2007). Root merger in Chinese compounds. *Studia Linguistica, 61*(2), 170–184.

Chapter 3
The Syntactic Structure of Mandarin V-V Resultatives: An Event-Mapping Approach

3.1 Introduction

In Chap. 2, I viewed resultative V-V compounds as complex words, that is, units at word level. Taking the two-domain hypothesis as a theoretical assumption, I proposed a syntactic analysis of the generation of the complex words of V-V resultatives. In this chapter, I further examine the syntactic structure of V-V resultatives in Mandarin from an event-mapping approach. I argue for a particular syntactic represention of the event/argument structure of V-V resultatives. This analysis provides evidence for syntactic decomposition of verbs into an array of syntactic heads.

In current generative linguistics, the syntactic representation of semantic event structure has become the mainstream approach to argument structure. Under this approach, the verbal/predicate semantics is decomposed into an event structure, which is represented by the syntactic structure. While it is generally agreed that the semantics/syntax interface is mediated by the event structure, researchers however disagree on how exactly syntax reflects and represents the semantic event structure. One stream of thought (e.g., Lin, 2004; Ramchand, 2008; Ritter & Rosen, 2000; Travis, 2010), the so-called isomorphism hypothesis, posits that syntax precisely mirrors the event structure through a correspondence relation between syntactic verbal projections (*v*Ps) and semantic (sub)events. On the other hand, some other authors (e.g., Pylkkänen, 2008; Marantz, 2013) argue that the correspondence relationship between the syntactic argument structure and the event structure is not a straightword one.

One widely cited work (to my knowledge, the only work) on the syntactic structure of V-V resultatives in Mandarin from an event-mapping approach is Lin (2004). Lin posits an inventory of three verbalizing heads, v_{DO}, v_{BECOME}, and v_{BE}, which represent three types of events, namely activity, inchoativety, and state; roots, which are category-nuetral, combine with these verbalizing heads as event modifiers. Mandarin has two types of V-V resultatiaves: object-oriented resultatives, in which the second verb is predicated of the object of the sentence, as in (1a), and subject-oriented resultatives, in which the second verb is predicated of the subject, as in (1b).

© The Author(s), under exclusive license to Springer Nature Singapore Pte Ltd. 2021   43
J. Liu, *The Syntax of V-V Resultatives in Mandarin Chinese*,
https://doi.org/10.1007/978-981-33-6846-0_3

(1) a. John **kan-dao**-le shu.   b. John **zou-lei**-le.
      John cut-fall-ASP tree   John walk-be.tired-ASP
      'John cut down a tree.'   'John walked and as a result got tired.'

Lin proposes an isomorphism analysis of Mandarin V-V resultatiaves, and claims that the two types of V-V resultatives have unified event structure and syntactic structure. Specifically, Lin argues that the event structure of the two types of V-V resultatives consists of three subevents, and correspondingly their syntactic structure contains three vPs, with each vP realizing one subevent. Taking (1a) as an example, Lin proposes that semantically (1a) is composed of three subevents: John's action of cutting, the tree's falling, and the final state of the tree being fallen. Lin argues that syntax generates three vPs to represent this event structure: a v_{DO}, merged with the root of the first verb *kan* 'cut', the null predicate v_{BECOME}, and v_{BE}, merged with the root of the second verb *dao* 'fall', as in (2).

(2)

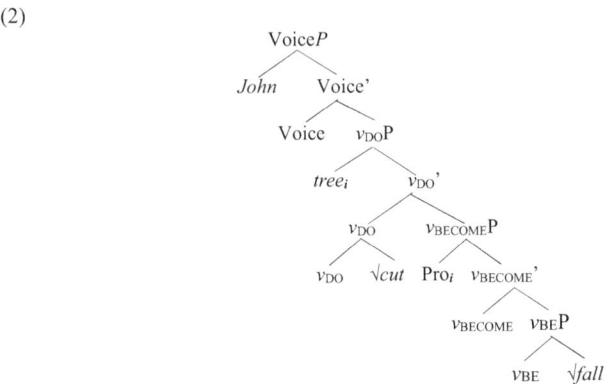

In this chapter, using adverbial modification properties to test the syntactic structure, I argue for the following points:

I. While V-V resultatives can be semantically analyzed as composed of three subevents (activity, change of state, final resultant state), the syntax does not generate three vPs (v_{DO}, v_{BECOME}, v_{BE}) in representing the event structure. That is, the isomorphism hypothesis does not hold.

II. For object-oriented resultatives, their syntactic structure contains two vPs; one conveys the interpreted meaning of CAUSE (v_{CAUSE}), and the other BECOME (v_{BECOME}). The root of the first verb $\sqrt{1}$ adjoins to v_{CAUSE} as a modifier denoting the manner of the causation, and the root of the second verb $\sqrt{2}$ merges with v_{BECOME} as a complement specifying the resultant state of the affected theme object.[1]

III. Subject-oriented resultatives are syntactically realized with a single v_{BECOME}P. That is, these resultatives are unaccusative predicates. In this syntactic structure, the v_{BECOME} head takes the root $\sqrt{2}$ as a complement, while $\sqrt{1}$ adjoins to the v_{BECOME} head as a modifier.

This analysis is illustrated in (3)–(4) below.

---

[1] Note that Lin's analysis does not distinguish the two types of head-root relations. In my analysis, I distinguish these two relations, as will be discussed in Sect. 3.4.

(3) a. Object-oriented resultatives
    John **kan-dao**-le shu.
    John cut-fall-ASP tree
    'John cut down a tree.'

b. Subject-oriented resultatives
    John **zou-lei**-le.
    John walk-be.tired-ASP
    'John walked and as a result got tired.'

(4) a. Object-oriented resultatives   b. Subject-oriented resultatives

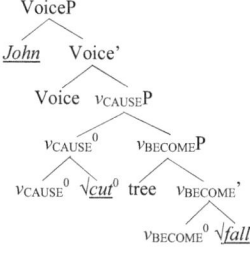

This chapter is organized as follows. Section 3.2 introduces the theoretical framework of my analysis, the event-mapping approach to argument structure. Specifically, in Sect. 3.2.1 I review two alternative approaches to argument structure: the lexicalist approach and the syntactic approach. In Sect. 3.2.2, I review the literature of the event-mapping approach to argument structure. I will first review event decomposition of verbal meanings (Sect. 3.2.2.1), and then I present various proposals on argument structure from the event-mapping approach (Sect. 3.2.2.2). In Sect. 3.3 I provide a review of previous analyses of V-V resultatives in Mandarin, and I introduce Lin's (2004) influential work in particular. After this preparatory work, I present my analysis in Sect. 3.4. In this section, I first focus on object-oriented resultatives (Sect. 3.4.1), and then consider subject-oriented resultatives (Sect. 3.4.2). Section 3.5 concludes this chapter.

3.2 The Event-Mapping Approach to Argument Structure

Argument structure is a central issue in generative linguistics, and two main approaches have been proposed: the lexicalist approach, which emphasizes the role of predicates such as verbs in projecting argument structures, and the syntactic approach, which posits that syntactic structures are generated autonomously, independent of the meaning of individual verbs. Within the framework of the syntactic approach to argument structure, it has been argued that syntax reflects relationships between events (such as causation and change of state) and the relationship between entities (event participants) and events, and the syntactic decomposition of event structure, or in another term, the event-mapping approach, has become a mainstream approach to argument structure (Lin, 2004; Marantz, 2013). In this section, I review the literature on the event-mapping approach to argument structure to contextualize my analysis, and also to present the theoretical assumptions that my analysis will adopt.

3.2.1   Lexicalist Versus Syntactic Approaches to Argument Structure

3.2.1.1   The Lexicalist Approach

An influential argument structure theory is characterized with the verb-centered approach, generally called *the lexicalist approach*. A fundamental assumption of this approach is that lexicon plays a central role in the interaction between form and meaning. This approach maintains that besides the sound-meaning pairing, the lexical entry of a verb also inherently contains the formal information of syntactic category and the number and type of arguments they require, which directly determines their argument structure (e.g., Bresnan, 1982; Di Sciullo & Williams, 1987; Jackendoff, 1975; Perlmutter, 1988). On this view, as Borer (2005) notes, verbs are "assumed to have fundamentally formal properties, which translate deterministically into a syntactic structure" (p. 3). The lexicalist approach to argument structure is anchored on the conception of thematic (semantic) roles (Fillmore, 1968), with the assumption that the mapping from argument structure to syntax is mediated by the thematic roles of arguments. The lexicalist approach hypothesizes that each verb bears an array of thematic roles, such as agent, patient, instrument, goal, etc., and a hierarchy of thematic roles governs the organization of arguments for each verb in syntax. On this view, the generation of the arguments of a verb is a matter of mapping the array of thematic roles to a syntactic representation according to certain linking rules. As part of this scheme, various linking rules are proposed, such as a theory of thematic hierarchies (e.g., Baker, 1988; Jackendoff, 1972). Under this approach, thematic roles are arranged in an abstract prominence hierarchy, and the syntactic realization of arguments is based on, and corresponds to, the position of thematic roles in this hierarchy. The central idea of the lexicalist approach, to summarize, is that verbs project their own argument structures based on their lexical specifications in combination with a thematic hierarchy.

3.2.1.2   The Syntactic Approach

In contrast to the lexicalist approach, the syntactic approach to argument structure posits that argument structures are generated independent of lexical demands (e.g., Borer, 2005; Halle & Marantz, 1993; Harley, 2011; Marantz, 1997, 2013; Pylkkänen, 2008; Schäfer, 2008; among others). The syntactic approach assumes that argument structures are a finite set of functional structures that are autonomously generated by grammar—structuresthe whose generation and existence do not depend on verbs and their meanings. Under the syntactic approach, individual verbs only choose to enter certain syntactic structures, and their function is to modify the meaning conveyed by these syntactic structures. I demonstrate this approach by reviewing two representative works, Hale & Keyser (1993) and Borer (2005).

In Hale & Keyser (1993), the argument structure of verbs is crucially reconcep-
tualized as syntactic configurations—rather than semantic or feature information
inherently stored in verbs. Hale & Keyser hypothesize that, for each category of
verbs, there exists a phrasal-level projection that represents their argument structure.
This phrasal projection establishes and defines a set of structural relations among its
components (head, specifier, and complement). Hale & Keyser crucially argue that
the semantic interpretations and syntactic properties of arguments are determined
by their positions in this projection and their relations to the other elements in this
structure. As an example, Hale & Keyser argue that the argument structure of the
verb *thin* as in *The cook thinned the gravy* is as in (5b).

(5) a. The cook thinned the gravy.

    b.

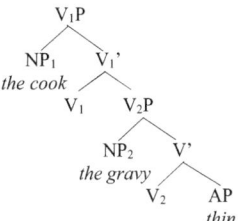

In Hale & Keyser's analysis, the verb *thin*—along with its two arguments, an agent
the cook, and a theme *the gravy*, has the argument structure in (5b), in which a matrix
VP (V$_1$P) embeds another VP (V$_2$P) as complement. To begin with, Hale & Keyser
propose that syntactic structures carry primitive meanings. Specifically, the meaning
associated with the structure of (5b)—a VP carrying another VP as complement—is
that the event denoted by V$_1$ implicates or causes the event denoted by the V$_2$. Based
on this, they further argue that the grammatical status of the NP$_1$ *the cook*, as the
subject of the sentence, is determined entirely by the syntactic relations it bears in
this structure, rather than by an agent thematic role it receives from the verb. To be
more specific, the interpretation of the subject argument *the cook* is determined by
two things: its structural position as the specifier of the upper VP in a double-VP
structure, and the interpreted CAUSE "elementary meaning" associated with this
structure. Hale & Keyser argue that it is in this light that the NP in the specifier of the
matrix VP is typically associated with the thematic role of agent. The grammatical
status of the DP$_2$ *the gravy* is likewise determined by its structural status—it occupies
the position of [SPEC, VP$_2$], which Hale & Keyser argue is the position in which
the theme role is generated and defined. In this framework, being the agent or the
theme means occupying the specifier position of the upper VP or of the embedded
VP, respectively.

By reconceptualizing argument structures as syntactic configurations, Hale &
Keyser's work implies the idea that syntax is generated independently of idiosyncratic
lexical requirements. In their analysis, a set of syntactic structures exist as part of
universal grammar. For example, the syntactic structure in (6a), in which a verb
carries a nominal complement, corresponds to the unergative verbs such as *laugh*,

sneeze, neigh, and *dance,* and also to the transitive verbs like *make* (as in *make trouble*), *have* (as in *have puppies*), and *do* (as in *do a jig*). Likewise, the structure in (6b) corresponds to location verbs such as *shelf*, and it is also the structure of verbs like *put*. That is to say, verbs do not project their own syntactic structures; rather, they are associated with certain independently generated syntactic structures.

(6) a.   b.

```
         V                                   V'
        / \                                  / \
       V   NP                               V   VP
           |                                   /  \
           N                                 NP    V'
                                                  / \
                                                 V   PP
                                                    / \
                                                   P   NP
                                                       N
```

Borer (2005) makes insightful observations on the autonomous syntax from two common phenomena. First, while lexical items demonstrate considerable flexibility in the interpretation of their meaning and in the frames where they can appear, the grammatical system, in contrast, is rigid, and imposes strict conditions on its interpretation. Borer provides the example of the English word *stone*. As a lexical item, *stone* can be used in various syntactic contexts and have different meanings; on the other hand, the properties and interpretations of the structures in which *stone* enters, such as *three stones*, *much stone*, or *to be stoned*, are rigid and strictly constrained. Second, some syntactic properties that are traditionally assumed to be determined by lexical items can be systematically overridden by the syntax. For example, according to the lexical approach, one property of the verb *stare* is that it is subcategorized as carrying a PP complement, as in (7a). However, the structure (7b), in which *stare* is directly followed by a DP, nonetheless is grammatical, even though the subcategorization requirement is violated.

(7) a. The alien stared at Kim.

  b. The alien stared Kim out of the room.

Borer argues that facts like these indicate that the grammatical system generates syntactic expressions, which get a semantic interpretation independent of the conceptual properties associated with the lexical items (roots). Borer maintains that lexical roots are fundamentally conceptualizations of world knowledge, not grammatical elements, and therefore are devoid of any syntactic properties, and are not responsible for the systematic aspects of the semantic interpretation of syntactic structures. Like Hale & Keyser (1993), Borer posits that argument structure—rather than being a matter of semantics inherently stored in the verb meaning—is actually a matter of the interpretation of DPs that appear in certain positions in a syntactic structure. It is the verbal phrase structure, in which (the root of) a verb enters and finds a position, that corresponds to the argument structure, not the properties of the verb root itself.

As just presented, both Hale & Keyser (1993) and Borer (2005) posit that syntax is generated automonously, independent of idiosyncratic lexical requirements. Note that together with this autonomous syntax view, these authors also assume that the autonomously generated syntactic structures carry interpreted meanings. As noted earlier, Hale & Keyser (1993) propose that syntactic structures convey "elementary meanings". Borer (2005) notes that the grammatical system generates syntactic expressions, which receive a semantic interpretation independent of the conceptual properties associated with the lexical roots. Marantz (2013) states that the meanings conveyed by verbal roots are separate from the meanings associated with the syntactic frames in which verbs appear. The idiosyncrasies in the meanings of verbal roots must be separated from the general, non-idiosyncratic connections between structure and meaning. That is, the syntactically representable meanings exist independent of any particular verbs. According to Marantz (2013), the function of the verb roots is to provide encyclopedic meaning to modify the meaning of syntactic structures. That is to say, verb roots play a "modificational, rather than constructive, role" (p. 160).

The syntactic approach to argument structure as reviewed above forms the general theoretical background and fundamental assumption of the present study. In my analysis of Mandarin V-V resultatives, I argue that the argument structure of the V-V resultatives is autonomously generated by the syntax, rather than projected by the two verb roots with their particular meanings; instead, the two verb roots integrate into the argument structure. In addition to this general assumption, I particularly assume the following two points.

First, in Hale & Keyser's (1993) proposal, the syntactic position for the theme is the specifier of the embedded VP. Note that in more recent theories, the notion of VP is replaced with vP, on the assumption that syntactically, a verb (i.e. VP in the earlier terms) is composed with a functional head little v and a root, and the little v and the root form a vP. Following Hale & Keyser's proposal, I will assume that the syntactic position of the theme object of Mandarin V-V resultatives is the specifier of the (embedded) vP that is associated with the change-of-state interpretation, which I label as v_{BECOME}P (more in Sect. 3.4).

Second, as for the introduction of the external argument, I will follow Kratzer (1996) and Pylkkänen (2008) and assume that it is introduced by a special functional head, Voice—rather than assuming that it occupies the specifier of an upper VP, as Hale & Keyser propose.

Within the framework of a syntactic approach to argument structure, I particularly adopt an event-mapping approach, which I review in the next section.

3.2.2 The Event-Mapping Approach to Argument Structure

3.2.2.1 Event-Structure Decomposition of Verbal Semantics

The notion event, generally speaking, refers to conceptions like causation, change, state, and time that figure in the grammar of human languages (Tenny & Pustejovsky, 2000). Vendler (1967) classifies verbal meanings into four types of events, given the inherent aspectual properties of their meanings: state, action, achievement, and accomplishment. Specifically, Vendler hypothesizes that verbs, given the inherent aspectual properties of their meanings, denote four types of events, namely, state, action, achievement, and accomplishment. In Vendler's classification, states have no internal structure or change during the time over which they are true (8a); an activity is an ongoing event with internal change and duration but no necessary temporal endpoint (8b); accomplishments are events with duration and an obligatory temporal endpoint (8c); achievements, on the other hand, have an instantaneous culmination or endpoint and are without duration (8d).

(8) a. John knows French.
    b. John walked for an hour yesterday.
    c. John painted a picture.
    d. John recognized that man.

Following early works such as Vendler (1967), an approach to verbal meanings has been developed that takes event and event structure as representational devices (e.g., Dowty, 1979; Pustejovsky, 1995; Ramchand, 2008; Rappaport Hovav & Levin, 1998; Tenny & Pustejovsky, 2000; van Hout, 1996). This approach is based on two core assumptions: first, key aspects of verbal/predicate meanings can be reduced to, and represented by, various types of events; second, events themselves have internal structure and can be decomposed into more primitive elements and the relations among these primitive elements. To demonstrate this approach, we can consider the sentence *John thinned the gravy*. From the event decomposition perspective, the verb phrase of this sentence expresses an accomplishment event, the thinning of the gravy by John. This event is composed of (at least) two subevents, an action of John thinning the gravy, and a change of state the gravy undergoes, as well as a causing relation between these two subevents. Thus, from the event decomposition approach, the semantics of the predicate of the sentence is represented by a structure in which an action causes a final state.

In modeling the event structure representation of verbal/predicate semantics, two different traditions have developed, which postulate different inventories of semantic primitives. One tradition, following Vendler (1967), views aspectual properties as the key to analyzing and representing predicate meaning. This approach classifies predicates on the basis of their aspectual properties, and decomposes predicates into subevents that are also aspectually defined. Ritter and Rosen (2000), for example, suggest that canonical events consist of temporal initiation, duration, and termination. Similarly, Ramchand (2008) proposes that predicate semantics is composed of the three events of initiation, process, and result. These authors posit that it is the temporal elements of events that are represented in grammar.

The other tradition decomposes predicate semantics into propositional or predicative primitives such as CAUSE, BECOME, and BE. McCawley (1968), for example, decomposes the meaning of the verb *kill* into a set of primitive predicates including CAUSE, BECOME, NOT ALIVE. Similarly, Carter (1976) represents the meaning of the verb *darken* with the structure [x CAUSE [[y BE DARK] CHANGE]]].

Along this line of decomposing lexical semantics into primitive predicates, one work of particular importance is Dowty (1979). Dowty proposes a way to represent Vendler (1967)'s four types of events with primitives like DO, CAUSE, and BECOME. In Dowty's system, the semantic primitives reflect the characterization of the different event types. As an example, Dowty's representation of an agentive accomplishment like *John sweeps the floor clean* is given in (9) below, in which a DO-ing event causes a BECOME-ing event.

(9) a. He sweeps the floor clean.

    b. [[DO(he, sweeps(the floor))] CAUSE [BECOME [clean(the floor)]]] (p. 123)

Traditionally, this representation of the verb meaning based on primitive predicates is also called *event structure*, and each primitive predicate is said to be a (sub)event. It should be noted that, this tradition, unlike the Vendlerian tradition, makes no direct ontological commitment to the aspectual properties of events.

The event-decomposition approach to lexical semantics has significant implications for theories of argument structures. Under this approach, argument structure can be represented via event structure, and the semantic roles borne by various verbal arguments can be conceptualized as event participants, with their realization and distribution governed by event structure. As Marantz (2013) states, "The syntax [...] reflect[s] relationships between events [...] and the relationship between entities and events must be projected onto a basic structure reflecting the events and their relations" (p. 4).

3.2.2.2 The Event-Mapping Approach to Argument Structure

As introduced in previous sections, theories on the syntactic approach to argument structure and on the event-structure decomposition of predicate semantics have reached two central conclusions:

I.   Verbal/predicate semantics can be decomposed into event structures.
II.   A set of universal argument structures, which reflect event structures, are autonomously generated in syntax.

Given these two general assumptions, a central issue in generative linguistics over the past decades is what these autonomously generated argument structures are, and how do they represent verbal/predicate event structures. While a variety of current proposals on argument structure share the two fundamental assumptions above, they nonetheless disagree in various respects. As stated earlier, one major controversy among current theories is how faithfully syntactic argument structure reflects the event structure. Some authors (e.g. Lin, 2004; Ramchand, 2008; Travis, 2010) argue that syntactic structure precisely mirrors event structure in a one-to-one correspondence relation between semantic (sub)events and syntactic *v*Ps. In contrast to these 'isomorphism' analyses, some other studies, for example, Marantz (2013) and Wood (2012), posit that, while argument structure represents event structure, this representation is not implemented through a pattern in which subevents necessarily correspond to subelements of syntactic structure—that is, syntactic structure does not precisely mirror event structure.

In this section, I review several proposals on argument structure, which I take to be representative of the literature. Specifically, I review Travis (2010), Ramchand (2008), and Lin (2004), three works that represent the isomorphism analysis. On the other hand, for the work that posits that there is no transparent correspondence relation between event structure and syntactic structure, I review Marantz (2013). Note that Travis (2010) and Ramchand (2008) are based on aspectually-defined events, while Lin (2004) adopts the tradition which decomposes events into primitive predicates. As my analysis adopts the primitive-predicates tradition of event decomposition like Lin (2004), I will provide a more detailed review of Lin's analysis, after briefly reviewing Travis (2010) and Ramchand (2008).

Travis (2010) and Ramchand (2008)

As a background of Travis' (2010) analysis, Pustejovsky (1995) proposes that accomplishments are composed of two subevents, an action process (P) and a final state (S), with the former causing the latter, a relaitoin Pustejovsky terms as *Transition* (T). This complex event structure is illustrated in (10a). Travis (2010) considers how the event structure of accomplishments proposed in Pustejovsky (1995) maps onto the double-VP configuration for verbal argument structure proposed in Larson (1988) and Hale & Keyser (1993), which is shown in (10b).

(10) a.   b.

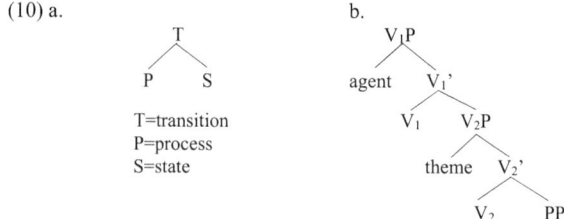

For Travis, there is a correspondence relation between these semantic subevents and syntactic VPs. Travis argues that the two subevents are represented as sub-VPs, with the upper VP (V_1P) representing the action event, and the inner VP (V_2P) indicating the resulting state.

The idea of aligning subevents—the causing event and final state in an accomplishment in particular—with the two VPs in argument structure is shared by other authors (e.g., Hoekstra, 1988; Mulder, 1992; Sybesma, 1992). It should be noted, however, that, while Travis argues that event structure is closely related to argument structure, she still assumes a lexical semantic representation independent of syntactic structure. This distinguishes her proposal from those of other authors, such as Ramchand (2008), and Lin (2004), who argue that event structure and syntactic structure are one and the same structure, as reviewed below.

Ramchand (2008) proposes an analysis that treats the event structure and the argument structure as one and the same structure. Following the literature (e.g., Grimshaw, 1990; Rappaport Hovav & Levin, 1998), Ramchand assumes that lexical items contain two types of meanings: structural meaning and lexical-encyclopedic content. Ramchand proposes that the process of constructing structural meanings is the process of syntactic event composition—the two processes are one and the same. Adopting an aspectually-defined notion of event, Ramchand views an event as a deconstruction built on the time dimension, from the initial point to the final state. Based on this, she identifies a set of primitive verbal meaning components, including *causation*, *change of state*, and *result*, and proposes that the structural meaning is constructed on the basis of these primitive semantic relationships. Specifically, Ramchand proposes that an event structure (maximally) contains three subeventive components: a causing subevent, a process-denoting subevent, and a subevent corresponding to a result state.

With regard to mapping the semantic event structure to the syntactic argument structure, Ramchand crucially proposes that the event structure, as a semantic representation, converges with the verbal argument structure as a syntactic representation, with each subevent being represented as its own syntactic projection, ordered in the hierarchical embedding relation. Specifically, Ramchand argues that the traditional VP domain is the locus where event structures are syntactically constructed. The event-based argument structure that Ramchand proposes is demonstrated in (11).

(11)

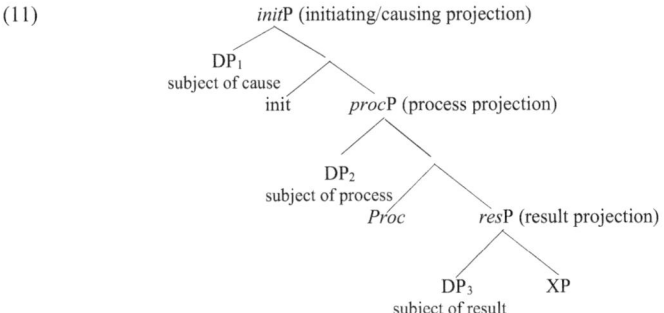

In (11), the *init*P introduces the causation event and the external argument (INITIATOR); *proc*P specifies the nature of the change or process and introduces the entity undergoing change or process (UNDERGOER); *res*P gives the telos or result state of the event and introduces the entity that comes to hold the result state (RESULTEE).

The key feature of Ramchand's analysis is the direct correlation between the verbal syntactic structure and the event structure. For Ramchand, the primitives such as causation, process, and result, have three identities: they are basic formatives for structural meanings, they are the primitive components for the event (de)composition, and they are also elements of VP syntactic structures (syntactic heads and projections).

Lin (2004)

Like Travis (2010) and Ramchand (2008), Lin (2004) posits a straightforward and transparent relation between event structure and verbal argument structure. Particularly, like Ramchand (2008), Lin argues that event structure is argument structure.

Unlike Travis (2010) and Ramchand (2008), however, Lin adopts the tradition that decomposes events into semantic primitives rather than aspectually-defined subevents (e.g., Carter, 1976; Dowty, 1979). In particular, following Dowty (1979), Lin proposes an inventory of three primitive predicates, namely, DO, BECOME, and BE, to represent the three event types of activity, change of state, and state. Following Marantz (1997), Lin assumes that verbs are not atomic units, but are syntactically formed with two components, a verbalizing head little *v*, and an acategorial root. The function of the verbalizing head is to syntactically categorize the root as a verb. Lin's analysis hypothesizes that verbalizing heads carry the meanings of the three primitives for event decomposition, DO, BECOME, and BE. In Lin's analysis, the categorizing head little *v* thus has two primary functions: it is a syntactic functional element, and it is also an event introducor.

Lin proposes three types of little *v*'s, v_{DO}, v_{BECOME}, v_{BE}, which represent activity, inchoativity, and stativity, respectively. According to Lin, a verb can denote a certain type of event because the little *v* it has carries the relevant corresponding primitive meaning. Lin assumes that activities and states are basic event types, and can be represented with a single primitive, DO or BE respectively. Achievements and accomplishments are complex events, which are built from the two basic events: achievements can be represented with a BECOME-BE structure, and accomplishments can be represented with the structure DO-BECOME-BE.

In Lin's analysis, activity predicates, such as *run* in *John ran* (12a), can be syntactically—and also semantically—represented as in (13a), in which the verbalizing head v_{DO} introduces an activity, and the root √run merges with little *v* as an event modifier. Likewise, state predicates such as *being tall* in *Mary is tall* (12b) can be represented as in (13b).

(12) a. John ran.   b. Mary is tall.

(13) a.   b.

Lin further proposes that the more complex change of state predicates such as *The window broke* in (14a) are formed by embedding a state v_{BE} under a v_{BECOME}, as demonstrated in (15a), while causative predicates such as *John broke the window* in (14b) are derived by adding a v_{DO} on top of a change of state predicate, as shown in (15b).

(14) a. The window broke.   b. John broke the window.

(15) a. change of state   b. causative

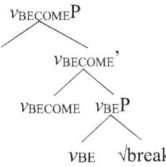 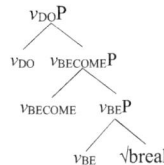

Lin's isomorphism hypothesis, to summarize, consists of two main points: semantic event structure and syntactic argument structure are the same structure; and complex event structures, as well as their syntactic representation, are formed by cascading the basic event/syntactic structures.

Marantz (2013)

In contrast to the isomorphism hypothesis, Marantz (2013) posits that, while argument structure represents event structure, this representation is not implemented through a pattern in which subevents necessarily correspond to subelements of syntactic structure—that is, syntactic structure does not precisely mirror event structure.

Marantz proposes that the core structure of a verb phrase contains a little *v* head and a root. The little *v* semantically introduces an eventuality, and the root modifies this event by contributing semantic content. In creating a *v*P structure, this little *v* head can (but does not necessarily) take a single complement. This single complement of the little *v* head can be a DP, as demonstrated in (16a), or it can be a predicative complement consisting of a DP subject and predicate (XP), which is traditionally called a *small clause*, as in (16b).

(16) a.   DP complement   b. small clause complement

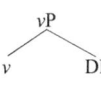   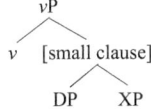

In Marantz's system, the lexical root plays a semantic modifying role, which is associated with the structural position it occupies. Specifically, a root can modify the event by merging with the little *v* (17a); or it can denote the state that is associated with a direct object of a change of state verb, and in this case it merges with the direct object (17b).[2]

---

[2]The tree structures are adapted from Manrantz (2013). Note that in this work, Marantz does not specifically clarify the nature or label of the phrase that is composed with the $\sqrt{}$(open) and the DP in (17b) and (18b).

(17)   a.   b.

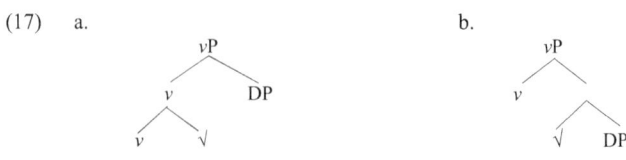

(Adapted from Marantz 2013, p.158)

To demonstrate the different distributions of roots, we consider two examples provided by Marantz. Marantz argues that in *John hammered the nail*, the verbal root √*hammer* modifies the event by imposing the manner of John's action, and it merges with little *v*, as in (18a). On the other hand, in the sentence *John opened the door*, the verbal root √*open* denotes the final state of the theme object *the door*, and it merges with the DP, as in (18b).

(18) a. John hammered the nail.   b. John opened the door.

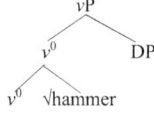   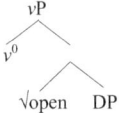

(Adapted from Marantz 2013, p.158)

Unlike Lin (2004), Marantz posits that the meaning conveyed by syntactic structure is not implemented by having the verbalizing head (little *v*) carry various primitive meanings; rather, it is a matter of the interpretation of the configuration in different contexts. According to Marantz, the canonical interpretation of the configuration of (16a), that is, the syntactic configuration in which a little *v* head carries a DP complement, is that a (dynamic) event is linguistically coded, and in this event, the DP undergoes a (caused) change of state. Marantz argues that the sentence *John opened the door*, for example, has this argument structure. In this structure, the little *v* introduces an event, the configuration conveys the change-of-state meaning, and *the door* is the theme that undergoes the change of state. The interpretation of the structure of (16b) is that the subject of the small clause undergoes a caused change of state to the state described by the predicate of the small clause, and this is the argument structure for sentences like *John put the book on the table*.

One central feature of Marantz's analysis is that there is no transparent relation between the argument structure and the event structure that it represents. As just mentioned, Marantz posits that the meaning conveyed by the syntactic structure—which is also the event structure—is not realized by positing semantic or event heads, such as CAUSE, in the syntax, but is the result of contextual interpretation of the structure, depending on the type of the complement of little *v* (i.e. DP or small clause), and on the position of the root. Marantz argues that there exists no one-to-one mapping relationship between the argument structure and the event structure, as is demonstrated by his analysis of the transitive use of *open*. In terms of semantics, an *opening* event would identify at least three subevents: a causing event, a change of state, and an end state; however, according to Marantz, in the argument structure for *open*, only one *v*P is projected, rather than three.

3.2.2.3 Assumptions of My Analysis

The event-based theory of the semantic/syntactic interface forms the theoretical framework for my analysis of the argument structure of Mandarin V-V resultatives. Based on these previous works, I assume the following points in my analysis.

First, I assume that semantic (sub)events are to some extent represented by syntactic *v*Ps. This assumption forms an important basis for my analysis. Based on this assumption, I will assume that adverbs which semantically modify (sub)events target *v*Ps in the syntactic structure.

Second, following Dowty (1979) and Lin (2004), I assume that event structures can be decomposed into meaning elements like CAUSE, DO, BECOME, and BE, and these primitive meanings are represented by, or associated with, little *v* heads. Note that there are different points of view in the literature as to whether verbalizing heads carry meanings. As mentioned earlier, Lin (2004) (along with other authors, such as Harley 2011) assumes that such heads carry meanings, while Marantz (2013) posits that the meaning associated with verbalizing heads is a matter of structural interpretation. In the present study, I use v_{CAUSE}, v_{BECOME}, and v_{BE} to refer to *v* heads that are associated with certain meanings, but I have nothing to say here about whether they inherently carry the relevant meaning, or whether it is instead the result of contextual interpretation of the structure.

While I do not completely adopt Marantz's system of argument structure, as I will demonstrate, his proposal that there is no precise one-to-one correspondence relation between semantic subevents and syntactic *v*Ps is supported in this work.

Before presenting my analysis in Sect. 3.4, I first review some previous studies on Mandarin V-V resultatives in the literature in the next section.

3.3   Previous Studies of V-V Resultatives in Mandarin

Resultative V-V compounds, especially their syntactic structure, have been a much-studied topic in the literature (e.g., Cheng & Huang, 1994; Her, 2007; Huang, 1992, 2006; Y. Li, 1990, 1993, 2005; H. Liu, 2004; Nishiyama, 1998; Tai, 2003; Zhang, 2001; Zou, 1994). Most of these previous studies do not take an event-mapping approach as presented in the last section. In other words, they do not examine the syntactic structure of V-V resultatives explicitly from the perspective of the syntactic representation of event structure; rather, these analyses focus on broader aspects of syntactic structure, largely in the framework of Government and Binding Theory. I call these previous studies *weakly decompositional analyses*. To my knowledge, Lin (2004) is the only analysis that takes an event-mapping approach. In what follows, I first briefly review several weakly decompositional analyses (Sect. 3.3.1), and then I review Lin's (2004) event-mapping analysis in greater detail (Sect. 3.3.2).

3.3.1 Weakly Decompositional Analyses of Mandarin V-V Resultatives

Weakly decompositional analyses of Mandarin V-V resultatives commonly propose a double-layered structure, in which a higher projection, normally a vP (in the sense of Chomsky, 1995), carries a complement XP. In this structure, the higher vP realizes the causing predicate denoted by V_1, and the complement XP realizes the resultative predicate denoted by V_2. These studies mainly differ in their analyses of the structure of the complement XP that represents V_2. Specifically, the resultative predicate (V_2P) has been analyzed, variously, as a VP (H. Liu, 2004; Nishiyama, 1998), a vP (Huang, 2006; Zhang, 2001), and a CP (Wang, 2010).

Nishiyama (1998), as introduced in Chap. 2 and repeated here, is typical of the analysis that treats the resultative predicate (V_2) in V-V resultatives as a VP. Applying Collins' (1997) structural representation of the Ewe SVC to Mandarin resultative compounds, Nishiyama (1998) proposes the structure in (19b) for the V-V resultative in (19a).

(19) a. Lisi **ku-shi**-le   shoujuan
         Lisi cry-be.wet-ASP handkerchief
         'Lisi cried and got the handkerchief wet.'

   b.

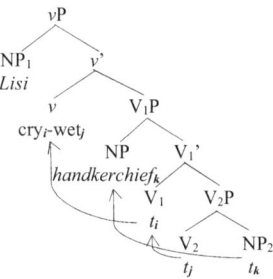

By contrast, Zhang (2001) follows the analysis of Hornstein and Lightfoot (1987) and Bowers (1993, 1997, 2000) that the phrase hosting a secondary predicate is a functional phrase. Zhang suggests that the functional phrase that hosts the resultative secondary predicate in Mandarin V-V resultatives is a vP, in which the little v head takes the V_2P as complement. The vP hosting the resultative predicate is in turn the complement of the primary predicate headed by V_1. Zhang's analysis distinguishes V-V resultatives in which the object is thematically selected by V_1 (20a), which she terms the *Transitive Resultative Construction* (TRC), and V-V resultatives in which the object bears no thematic relation to V_1 (20b), which she terms the *Intransitive Resultative Construction* (IRC).

(20) a. Akiu **da-si**-le   laohu.
       Akiu beat-die-ASP tiger
       'Akiu beat and killed the tiger.'

    b. Akiu **ku-shi**-le   shoujuan.
       Akiu cry-be.wet-ASP handkerchief
       'Akiu cried and as a result the handkerchief was wet.'

Zhang argues that, in Mandarin, TRCs and IRCs have different syntactic structures: while in TRCs, the affected argument (the DP appearing after the V-V compound) is the object of V_1, it is the subject of V_2 in IRCs. Zhang further argues that, in TRCs, the affected argument controls a PRO subject of the resultative predicate. IRCs, in contrast, have an ECM structure and no PRO is involved; instead, the subject of the secondary resultative predicate raises into the matrix predicate for case checking. Specifically, Zhang proposes that Mandarin TRCs such as (21a) have the syntactic structure in (21b).

(21) a. Akiu **da-sui**-le   nage huaping.
       Akiu hit-break-ASP that vase
       'Akiu broke that vase by hitting it.'

    b.

In this structure, the resultative predicate verb *sui* 'break' first raises to the lower *v*, and it then moves further to the right of the V_1 *da* 'hit', which selects the lower *v*P as complement. Then the newly formed compound *da-sui* 'hit-break' raises to ASP, deriving the surface sequence.

Unlike Nishiyama (1998) and Zhang (2001), Wang (2010) argues that V-V resultatives are bi-clausal constructions, in which the embedded resultative predication projects a CP, as demonstrated in (22a, b).

(22) a. Lisi **da-si**-le   na-zhi   zhanglang.
          Lisi hit-die-ASP that-CL cockroach
          'Lisi hit that cockroach and (as a result) it died.'

   b.

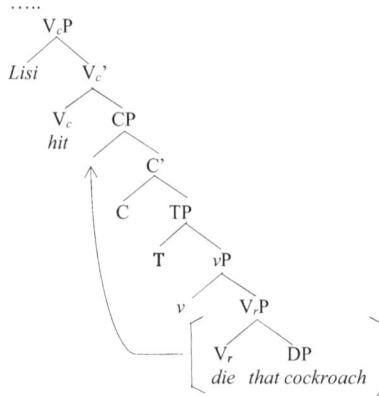

Wang argues that the affected argument is the internal argument of V_2, but this argument gets Case assigned from V_1. Wang claims that, in order for this internal argument of V_2 to acquire its case, it has to raise to a higher functional position so that it is accessible to the functional domain of V_1. Wang's analysis crucially invokes the smuggling analysis of Collins (2005).[3] Specifically, Wang (2010) proposes that V_2P as a whole moves to the specifier of the embedded CP, and the internal argument, pied-piped with this VP movement, is smuggled to an edge position of a strong phase, where it can receive case from the matrix V_1. (22a) and the corresponding tree in (22b) demonstrate this analysis.

The three authors above propose different syntactic structures for V-V resultatives in Mandarin. Notably, in these studies, the argument structure and its generation are not examined from the perspective of syntactic representation of event structures. In the next section, I review an alternative approach, the event-mapping approach of Lin (2004).

---

[3]Collins (2005) proposes the smuggling analysis in a study of raising constructions in English such as (i).

   (i) *John seems to Mary to be nice.*

   Collins notes that given the Minimal Link Condition (MLC), one issue that (i) raises is why the NP *Mary* does not block movement of DP *John* from the embedded clause to the matrix subject position. Collins proposes that this is because a VP movement 'smuggles' the embedded subject *John* to pass the experiencer *Mary*, thus avoiding a violation of the MLC. Collins (2005) provides the following definition for *smuggle*: 'suppose that there is a constituent YP which contains XP, and XP is inaccessible to Z due to existence of some intervening W (which is a strong phase boundary). The intervening W blocks a syntactic relation between Z and XP. However, if YP moves to a higher position, it can be said that XP is smuggled by the YP to a position higher than W' (p. 292).

3.3.2 Lin (2004): An Event-Mapping Approach

Although the event-mapping approach to argument structure has become a mainstream approach in current generative linguistics, studies of the argument structure of Mandarin V-V resultatives from this approach are few—actually, Lin (2004) is the only such study to my knowledge. As just introduced, Lin posits that event structure is syntactic argument structure, and that syntactic verbalizing heads are event introducers. Lin proposes three types of little v's, v_{DO}, v_{BECOME}, and v_{BE}, which represent activity, inchoative, and state, respectively. In this way, the process by which verbal argument structure is generated is also the process by which verb meanings are compositionally constructed from conceptual primitives.

Lin considers two types of V-V resultatives in Mandarin: object-oriented resultatives, in which V_2 is predicated of the theme object, and subject-oriented resultatives, in which V_2 is predicated of the subject. (23a) is an example of object-oriented resultative, as V_2 *dao* 'fall' is predicated of the theme object *shu* 'tree'; (23b) is a subject-oriented resultative, where V_2 *si* 'die' is predicated of the subject *wo* 'I'.

(23) a. Object-oriented V-V resultatives   b. Subject-oriented V-V resultatives

John **kan-dao**-le shu.	wo **xiao-si**-le.
John cut-fall-ASP tree	I laugh-die-ASP
'John cut down a tree.'	'I laughed myself to death.'

In Lin's analysis, object-oriented and subject-oriented resultatives have a unified event structure—in both cases, an activity causes an achievement event. Corresponding to this event structure, Lin proposes a three-layered verbal argument structure: a v_{DO} head takes a $v_{BECOME}P$ as complement, which in turn takes a $v_{BE}P$ as complement. In this structure, the roots of V_1 and V_2 merge with the v_{DO} head and v_{BE} head respectively, as event modifiers. As an example, Lin proposes the structures in (24a, b) for the two resultatives in (23a, b) respectively. As for the external argument, Lin assumes that it is introduced by the functional head Voice.

(24) a.   b.

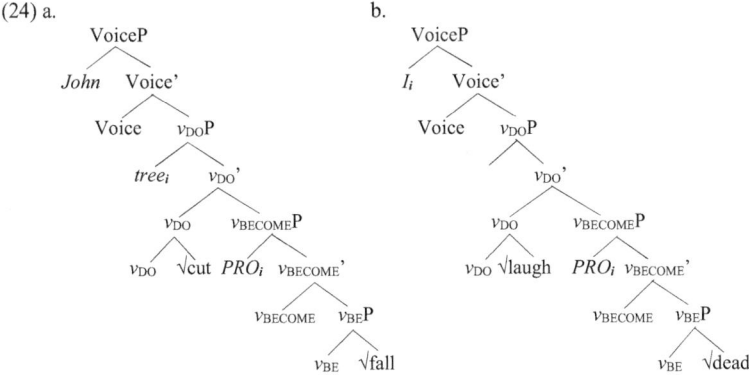

The key feature of Lin's analysis is that the syntax projects three vP's to realize the three semantic subevents. Specifically, V_1, which denotes the causing event, corresponds to the v_{DO}P, and V_2, which denotes the resultant state, corresponds to a v_{BE}P. In the next section, I present my analysis of the two types of V-V resultatives in Mandarin.

3.4 Syntactic Structure of V-V Resultatives in Mandarin: The Evidence from Adverbial Modification Properties

In this section, I present my analysis of the syntactic structure of V-V resultatives in Mandarin. Specifically, I explore the syntactic structure of V-V resultatives by examining their adverbial modification properties. In the present analysis, I assume the verbalizing head semantically represents the primitive meanings of causation, activity, inchoativity, and stativity, and I use v_{CAUSE}, v_{DO}, v_{BECOME}, and v_{BE} respectively to refer to the verbalizing head with the semantic interpretation indicated by the subscript. Following Lin (2004), I assume that both object-oriented and subject-oriented V-V resultatives in Mandarin convey the basic semantics of activity > change of state > final state. Starting from this assumption, my focus is to determine how this semantic event structure is syntactically represented. To be more specific, I aim to determine what vPs are projected in the syntactic structure of Mandarin V-V resultatives.

The test of adverbial modification has long been used to investigate how events are represented in syntactic structures, and it is generally assumed that adverbs modify only events with some syntactic representation (Harley, 2011; Kyle & Beck, 2004; Marantz, 2013; Pylkkänen, 2008; von Stechow, 1996). It is also assumed that certain adverbs, such as manner advers and agentive adverbs, and so forth, syntactically are vP adjuncts, that is, adverbs target vPs (cf. Marantz, 2013). Following this research line, in the present analysis, I assume that, when adverbs that normally modify a certain type of vP—representing a certain meaning such as causation, activity, inchoativity, or stativity—can occur in a sentence, this type of vP is present in the syntactic structure of the sentence, and vice versa.

Based on the adverbial modification properties of V-V resultatives, I make the following two main claims: first, while V-V resultatives can be semantically analyzed as composed of three subevents (activity > change of state > final state), the syntax does not generate three vPs (v_{DO} > v_{BECOME} > v_{BE}) in representing their event structure; secondly, object-oriented V-V resultatives and subject-oriented V-V resultatives have different syntactic structures. Specifically, in object-oriented resultatives, the syntax generates two vPs: v_{CAUSE}P, and v_{BECOME}P. The root of the first verb ($\sqrt{1}$) adjoins to v_{CAUSE} as a modifier denoting the manner of the causation; the root of the second verb ($\sqrt{2}$) merges with v_{BECOME} as a complement specifying the resultant state of the object of the sentence. By contrast, subject-oriented resultatives are syntactically realized with a single v_{BECOME}P. In this structure, the v_{BECOME} head takes the root $\sqrt{2}$ as a complement, while $\sqrt{1}$ adjoins to the v_{BECOME} head as a manner modifier.

In the rest of this section, I consider first object-oriented V-V resultatives (Sect. 3.4.1), and then subject-oriented V-V resultatives (Sect. 3.4.2). For each type of V-V resultatives, I examine their adverbial modification properties by considering three questions: What adverbs can modify V_1? What adverbs can modify V_2? What adverbs can modify both V_1 and V_2 ($V_1 + V_2$)?

3.4.1 The Syntactic Structure of Object-Oriented V-V Resultatives

Briefly speaking, object-oriented V-V resultatives in Mandarin demonstrate the following adverbial modification properties: some adverbs modify V_1, some modify V_2, and some modify both V_1 and V_2 ($V_1 + V_2$). I first consider adverbial modification involving V_1, providing evidence for the presence of the v_{CAUSE} head and the absence of the v_{DO} head.

3.4.1.1 The Evidence for $v_{CAUSE}P$

As noted earlier, I assume that, in simplex activities such as (25a), a $v_{DO}P$ is projected in the syntactic structure, as illustrated in (25b). I also assume that adverbs that modify a simplex activity predicate are v_{DO} adverbs.

(25) a. John zoulu.   b.
         John walk $v_{DO}P$
         'John walked.'   ╱╲
                                                        v_{DO} $\sqrt{}$walk

If we adopt the isomorphism analysis, we would expect that v_{DO} adverbs that modify V_1 as a simplex activity predicate should be able to modify V_1 in an object-oriented V-V resultative, and conversely, adverbs that modify V_1 in object-oriented V-V resultatives should be able to modify V_1 as a simplex predicate. However, a close examination of the various V_1 adverbial modification patterns indicates that this is not always the case, as demonstrated below.

First, when verbs function as a simplex activity predicates, as in the usual case, they can be modified by certain adverbs, typically manner adverbs, as is shown in (26a); however, when the same verbs function as the V_1 of object-oriented V-V resultatives, they can no longer be modified by this class of adverbs, as shown in (26b). That is to say, simplex activity V modifiers cannot function as V_1 modifiers in V-V resultatives. I refer to this adverbial modification pattern as *Pattern I*.

(26) a. John zai   dashengde **ku**.
      John PROG loudly   cry
      'John is crying loudly.'

   b. John (*dashengde) **ku-shi**-le   shoujuan.
      John   loudly   cry-be.wet-ASP handkerchief
      Intended meaning: 'John cried loudly and as a result his handkerchief got wet.'

In (26a), the action verb *ku* 'cry', when functioning as a simplex activity predicate, can be modified by manner adverbs like *dashengde* 'loudly'. However, when *ku* 'cry' functions as V_1 of an object-oriented resultative, the adverb *dashengde* 'loudly' is not possible (26b). The example in (27) illustrates the same phenomenon.

(27) a. John (zai)   anjingde **kan** (shu).
      John PROG quietly   read (book)
      'John is reading quietly.'

   b. John (*anjingde) **kan-hua**-le   yanjing.
      John   quietly   read-be.blurred-ASP eye
      Intended meaning: 'John read too much quietly and his eyes got blurred.'

Pattern I indicates that activity modifiers, at least in certain cases, cannot occur in object-oriented V-V resultatives to modify V_1, which semantically denotes an activity event.

Second, some manner adverbs can normally modify a simplex activity V, as in (28a); however, when they appear in V-V causatives, they are forced to be interpreted as modifying the whole V-V compound, and cannot be interpreted as modifying V_1 only, as shown in (28b). I refer to this adverbial modification pattern as *Pattern II*.

(28) a. John butingde   **tui**   na-shan men.
      John repeatedly push that-CL door
      'John repeatedly pushed that door.'

   b. John butingde   **tui-kai**   na-shan men.
      John repeatedly push-open that-CL door
      √ 'John repeatedly pushed that door open.'
      *'John (finally) got that door open by repeatedly pushing on it.'

In (28a), the adverb *butingde* 'repeatedly' modifies the simplex activity verb *tui* 'push'; when *butingde* 'repeatedly' occurs in an object-oriented resultative, as in (28b), however, it cannot be interpreted as modifying just V_1 *tui* 'push', but modifies the whole V-V resultative. A similar example is given in (29).

(29) a. John (zai)   feikuaide   **pao**.
      John (PROG) fast/quickly run
      'John is running very fast/quickly.'

   b. John feikuaide   **pao-diu**-le xiezi.
      John fast/quickly   run-lost-ASP shoe
      √ 'Quickly, John got off his shoes by/in running.'
      *'John ran very fast, and (as a result) he lost his shoes.'

Pattern II further indicates that simplex V modifiers cannot occur in object-oriented resultatives as V_1 modifiers alone.

Thirdly, while some manner adverbs seem to be able to modify the V_1 of object-oriented resultatives, they cannot modify the same verb functioning as a simplex activity predicate, as indicated in (30) and (31). In (30a), the manner adverb *yijiao* 'with one kick' modifies V_1 *ti* 'kick'; however, as indicated in (30b), it cannot modify the simplex activity verb *ti* 'kick'. Likewise, while the manner adverb *san-quan liang-jiao* '(with) a couple of strikes' seems to modify V_1 *da* 'beat' in an object-oriented resultative, it cannot modify the verb functioning as a simplex activity predicate. I refer to this adverbial modification pattern as *Pattern III*.

(30) a. John <u>yijiao</u>   **ti-kai**-le   men.
        John one.kick kick-open-ASP door
        'John kicked the door open with (just) one kick.'

    b. *John <u>yijiao</u>   **ti**   men.
        John one.kick kick door

(31) a. John <u>san-quan liang-jiao</u> jiu   **da-si**-le   laohu.
        John three.fist two.kick [only] beat-die-ASP tiger
        'John beat the tiger to death with just a couple of strikes.'

    b. *John san-quan liang-jiao **da**   laohu.
        John three.fist two.kick beat tiger

Finally, we consider the situation in which adverbs do seem to be able to modify both simplex activity V and V_1 in object-oriented resultatives. Some adverbs, in particular, agentive adverbs, such as *yonglide* 'forcefully', *shengqide* 'angrily', but also other manner adverbs, such as *qingqingde* 'lightly, gently', can modify both simplex activity V and V_1 in object-oriented resultatives, as is illustrated in (32)–(34). I call this adverbial modification pattern *Pattern IV*.

(32) a. John zhengzai <u>yonglide/shengqide</u> **tui**   na-shan men.
        John PROG   forcefully/angrily   push that-CL door
        'John was pushing that door forcefully/angrily.'

    b. John <u>yonglide</u> /shengqide **tui-kai**   na-shan men.
        John forcefully/angrily   push-open that-CL door
        'John pushed that door forcefully/angrily and got it open.'

(33) a. John (zai)   <u>dakoudakoude</u> **chi** (fan).
        John PROG with.big.bite   eat food
        'John is eating with big bites.'

    b. John <u>dakoudakoude</u> **chi-guang**-le   wanlide   fan.
        John with.big.bite   eat-be.clean-ASP in.the.bowl food
        'John ate up the food in the bowl with big bites.'

(34) a. feng zai   <u>qingqingde</u> **chui**.
        wind PROG lightly   blow
        'The wind is blowing lightly.'

    b. feng <u>qingqingde</u> **chui-qi-le**   na-pian shuye.
        John lightly   blow-rise that-CL leaf
        'The wind blew up that leaf lightly.'

Under the assumption that V_1 in object-oriented resultatives projects a $v_{DO}P$ as Lin proposes, we face a dilemma: Pattern IV seems to indicate that V_1 is modified by v_{DO} modifiers; the other three patterns, however, indicate that V_1 in object-oriented resultatives cannot be modified by v_{DO} modifiers. In other words, while Pattern IV supports the view that V_1 projects a $v_{DO}P$, Pattern I, II, and III indicate the opposite. Based on these adverbial modification facts, I make the proposals in (35), putting aside $v_{BECOME}P$ and $v_{BE}P$ for the moment.

(35) i. In object-oriented V-V causatives, syntax generates not a $v_{DO}P$, but a $v_{CAUSE}P$, and the root of V_1 is a modifier of the v_{CAUSE} head.

   ii. All the surface V_1 modifiers actually modify the $v_{CAUSE}P$; syntactically these modifiers have no access to (the root of) V_1 and therefore cannot modify it.

The tree structure in (36) below represents this proposal.

(36)

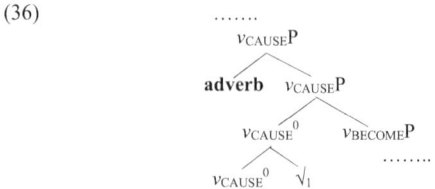

This analysis is in the same spirit as Pylkkänen's (2008) analysis of direct causatives in English. In English direct causatives, taking *awake* as an example, an adverb such as *grumpily* can only modify the causing event but not the caused event, as illustrated in (37a).

(37) a. John awoke Bill grumpily.   b. vP
      (false if John wasn't grumpy)

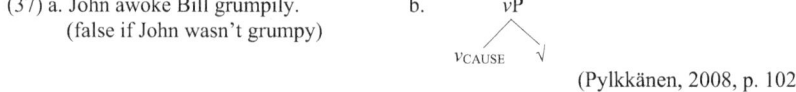

                                                  (Pylkkänen, 2008, p. 102)

In accounting for why the adverb in such constructions cannot modify the caused event, Pylkkänen proposes the structure in (37b). In this structure, a v_{CAUSE} head takes as its complement a root that denotes the caused event. Given the assumption that adverbs modify vP, the adverbs will be adjoined only after the root has merged with the v_{CAUSE} head, so the adverbs can modify only the causing event, not the root.

I propose that a variant of this analysis of English direct causatives from Pylkkänen also captures the complex V_1 adverbial modification properties of Mandarin object-oriented V-V resultatives. As illustrated in (36), I propose that a v_{CAUSE} head takes as a modifier the root of V_1, which semantically indicates an action event. As the adverbs modify $v_{CAUSE}P$ and have no access to the root of V_1, semantically they can only modify the CAUSE meaning. In what follows, I will demonstrate how the adverbial modification facts follow from this syntactic structure.

Let us consider Pattern I first. Pattern I indicates that v_{DO} modifiers cannot occur in object-oriented V-V resultatives. In my analysis, the syntactic structure of these resultatives does not project $v_{DO}P$, but instead projects a $v_{CAUSE}P$. This explains why simplex V_1 modifiers cannot occur in V-V causatives. In the example (26) repeated as (38) below, while the adverb *dashengde* 'loudly' can modify the activity predicate *ku* 'cry', it is unacceptable for it to modify v_{CAUSE}P to make the meaning that 'John, in a loud way, caused the handkerchief to be wet' by crying, which is semantically and pragmatically odd.

(38) a. John zai   dashengde   **ku**.
    John PROG loudly   cry
    'John is crying loudly.'

   b. John (*dashengde) **ku-shi**-le   shoujuan.
     John   loudly   cry-be.wet-ASP handkerchief
     Intended meaning: 'John cried loudly and as a result his handkerchief got wet.'

Pattern II can also receive a straightforward explanation. In (39), repeated from (28), the adverb *butingde* 'repeatedly' semantically and syntactically can modify either the DO meaning in (39a) or the CAUSE meaning in (39b). This adverb can no longer modify V_1 alone in (39b) because there is no v_{DO}P generated.

(39) a. John butingde   **tui**   na-shan men.
    John repeatedly push that-CL door
    'John repeatedly pushed that door.'

   b. John butingde   **tui-kai**   na-shan men.
    John repeatedly push-open that-CL door
    √'John repeatedly pushed that door open.'
    *'John got that door open by repeatedly pushing on it.'

Pattern III can be explained in the same way. Given its meaning, the adverb *yijiao* '(with) one kick' in (40) repeated from (30) can naturally modify the CAUSE meaning, but not the DO meaning, and that is why it can occur in (40a) but not in (40b).

(40) a. John yijiao   **ti-kai**-le   men.
    John one.kick kick-open-ASP door
    'John kicked the door open with just one kick.'

   b. *John yijiao   **ti**   men.
    John one.kick kick door

The adverb *yijiao* '(with) one kick', actually does not describe the manner that John made the kick, but describes the manner that John caused the door to open by kicking it.

The argument that adverbs like *yijiao* '(with) one kick' and *san-quan-liang-jiao* '(with) a couple of strikes' modify the CAUSE meaning rather than the DO meaning is further supported by object-oriented resultatives in which the V_1 is a light verb without definite meaning, as in (41).

(41) a. John san-xia-liang-xia   jiu ba men **da-kai**-le.
    John three.strike.or.two.strike only BA door beat-open-ASP
    John got the door open with just a couple of strikes.

  * b. John san-xia-liang-xia   **da** men.
    John three.strike.or.two.strike beat door

In (41a), V_1 *da* has the literal meaning of 'to beat, to hit'. In this sentence, *da* does not have its literal meaning, but simply expresses the meaning of 'somehow cause/get (the door to open)'. If the adverb *san-xia-liang-xia* '(with) two or three strikes' is analyzed as modifying the DO meaning, the literal meaning of V_1, this sentence is ill-formed, like (41b). Therefore, a better analysis is that the adverb modifies v_{CAUSE}, denoting the manner in which John caused the door to open, rather than how John 'beat' the door, which is pragmatically odd.

Having demonstrated that the first three adverbial modification patterns provide evidence for the analysis that V-V resultatives contain a v_{CAUSE} head rather than a v_{DO} head, now we consider Pattern IV, in which simplex activity V_1 (v_{DO}) modifiers do seem to be able to occur in V-V resultatives to modify V_1, therefore challenging the proposed analysis. I repeat the two examples of Pattern IV in (42) and (43) below.

(42) a. John zhengzai <u>yonglide</u>   **tui**   na-shan men.
         John PROG   forcefully push that-CL door
         'John was pushing that door forcefully.'

   b. John <u>yonglide</u>   **tui-kai**-le   na-shan men.
      John forcefully push-open-ASP that-CL door
      'John pushed that door forcefully and got it open.'

(43) a. John (zai)   <u>dakoudakoude</u>   **chi** (fan).
         John PROG with.big.bite   eat food
         'John is eating with big bites.'

   b. John <u>dakoudakoude</u>   **chi-guang**-le   wanlide   fan.
      John with.big.bite   eat-be.clear-ASP in.the.bowl food
      'John ate up the food in the bowl with big bites.'

Pattern IV raises this question: when occurring in object-oriented resultatives, do these adverbs modify v_{CAUSE}, or v_{DO}? I argue that, in these examples, the adverbs modify v_{CAUSE}, not v_{DO}.

First, note that adverbs such as *yonglide* 'forcefully' and *dakoudakoude* 'with big bites' are semantically compatible with the meaning CAUSE (in addition to DO), as indicated in (44). That is, semantically they can be v_{CAUSE} modifiers.

(44) a. John <u>yonglide</u>   **shi**   na-shan da   men kai-le   yi-tiao feng.
         John forcefully make/cause that-CL huge door open-ASP one-CL crack
         'John made the door open a few inches forcefully.'

   b. John <u>dakoudakoude</u>   **shi**   wanlide   fan jian-le   di
      John with.big.bites make/cause in.the.bowl food show-ASP bottom
      'John made the bowl empty of food with big bites.'
      [Literal meaning: John ate up all the food in the bowl with big bites so that made the
             bowl show its bottom.]

Second, we consider the adverb *dakoudakoude* 'with big bites' as in the example in (45). Interestingly, unlike (43b), (45) is ill-formed. If we assume that the adverb *dakoudakoude* 'with big bites' modifies a v_{DO} in the V-V resultative, the ill-formedness of (45) is difficult to explain.

(45) John (*<u>dakoudakoude</u>) **chi-qiong**-le   ta fuqin.
    John with.big.bites eat-be.poor-ASP his father
    Intended meaning: 'John got his dad poor by eating with big bites.'

Based on the observations above, I conclude that, in Pattern IV of adverb modification, the adverbs modify v_{CAUSE}, not v_{DO}.

What, then, accounts for the contrast between (43b) and (45), which I repeat in (46) below? That is, why can the same adverb *dakoudakoude* 'with big bites' occur in one object-oriented V-V resultative (46a), but not in another (46b)? I here propose a pragmatic explanation.

(46) a. John <u>dakoudakoude</u> **chi-guang**-le   wanlide   fan.
      John with.big.bites eat-be.clear-ASP in.the.bowl food
      'John ate up the food in the bowl with big bites.'

    b. John (*<u>dakoudakoude</u>) **chi-qiong**-le   ta fuqin.
      John   with.big.bites eat-be.poor-ASP his father
      Concervable meaning: 'John made his dad poor by eating with big bites.'

First, I hypothesize that, in certain cases, activity-modifying adverbs (i.e. v_{DO} modifiers) can occur in resultatives—to modify the v_{CAUSE} head. Based on the data that I observed in this study, it seems true that, in object-oriented resultatives, the process of V$_1$ action is the causing process for the result denoted by V$_2$. We demonstrate this by considering the situation that *John cut down a tree*: we can say that the process of John's cutting action is also the process of causing the tree to fall by John. Based on this claim, I propose that the adverbs modifying the action can usually occur in resultatives to modify the causing event, if they are semantically and pragmatically compatible. Pragmatically it is possible that the manner or state in which the subject conducts the action denoted by V$_1$ can also be (perceived as) the manner or state in which the subject causes the final state of the theme object. Consider the examples in (47). In (47a, b), repeated from (42), the process of John pushing the door hard co-occurs with the process of John causing the door to open. Actually, the two processes are one and the same process. I propose that it is due to this relation between the V$_1$ action and the causing process that the action-modifying adverb such as *yonglide* 'forcefully' can also occur in V-V resultatives. The modification of the adverb *dakoudadkoude* '(with) big bites' in (47c, d), repeated from (43), can receive a similar analysis.

(47) a. John zhengzai <u>yonglide</u> **tui**   na-shan men.
     John PROG   forcefully push that-CL door
     'John was pushing that door forcefully.'

   b. John <u>yonglide</u> **tui-kai**   na-shan men.
     John forcefully push-open that-CL door
     'John pushed on that door forcefully and got it open.'

   c. John (zai)   <u>dakoudakoude</u> **chi** (fan).
     John PROG with.big.bites   eat food
     'John is eating with big bites.'

   d. John <u>dakoudakoude</u> **chi-guang**-le   wanlide   fan.
     John with.big.bites   eat-be.clear-ASP in.the.bowl food
     'John ate up the food in the bowl with big bites.'

On the other hand, at least for some object-oriented V-V resultatives—probably due to pragmatic reasons—the physical process of the V_1 activity is not perceived as the same as the causing process. I argue that in this case, the v_{DO} modifiers cannot occur in resultatives, since they are unable to modify the v_{CAUSE} head. I propose that the modification of the adverb *dakoudadkoude* '(with) big bites' in (48), repeated from (46b), is such a case.

(48) John (*<u>dakoudakoude</u>) **chi-qiong**-le   ta fuqin.
     John   with.big.bites   eat-be.poor-ASP his father
     Intended meaning: 'John made his dad poor by eating with big bites.'

In (48), John making his father poor by eating is normally a gradual process, and it is pragmatically odd to imply that, with each bite, his father gets a little bit poorer. That is, the process of getting his father poor does not exactly co-occur with each step of the physical bites. In this case, this adverb cannot modify the CAUSE meaning, and that is why it cannot occur in object-oriented V-V resultatives.

To sum up, through adverbial modification properties, I have argued that, in object-oriented V-V resultatives, a v_{CAUSE} head is projected, but not a v_{DO} head. In the next subsection, I consider the adverbial modification of V_2 in this construction, and argue that a v_{BECOME} head is present in the syntactic structure of these constructions.

3.4.1.2   *The Evidence for the $v_{BECOME}P$*

Adverbial modification involving V_2 in object-oriented V-V resultatives demonstrates two patterns, both providing argument for the existence of a separate v_{BECOME} head.

The first pattern is that adverbs such as *yijing* 'already', *mashang* 'immediately', *like* 'immediately', *manmande* 'slowly', *xunshude* 'quickly', modify both V_1 (v_{CAUSE} in the present analysis) and V_2, as illustrated in (49). Following the literature (e.g., Bonami, Godard, & Manhe, 2004), I call this group of adverbs *time adverbs*.

(49) a. John <u>manmande</u>/<u>xunsude</u>/<u>yixiazi</u>   /<u>mashang</u>   **tui-kai**-le   men.
John slowly   /quickly /all.of.a.sudden /immediately push-open-ASP door
'John slowly/quickly/all of a sudden/immediately pushed the door open.'

b. qiufeng <u>yijing</u> /<u>manmande</u>/<u>yiyezhijian</u>   **chui-huang**-le   shuye.
fall.wind already/slowly   /over.a.single.night blow-yellow-ASP leaf
'The fall wind already/slowly/over a single night turned the leaves yellow.'

In these examples, both V_1 and V_2 fall in the modifying scope of the adverbs. We take *manmande* 'slowly' as an example, as shown in (50). With the adverb *manmande* 'slowly', the interpretation of (50) is that John, in a slow manner, caused the door to open by pushing it. Given this interpretation, and also considering that the adverb *manmande* 'slowly' is semantically compatible with the CAUSE meaning, I propose that the adverb in this sentence modifies a v_{CAUSE} head. Notably, (50) also conveys the meaning that the door became open in a slow manner; it cannot mean that John pushed (a button of) the door slowly, and somehow the door opened quickly, a scenario which is pragmatically possible. Based on this, I conclude that the adverb *manmande* 'slowly' also modifies V_2.

(50) a. John <u>manmande</u> **tui-kai**-le   men.
John slowly   push-open-ASP door
√ 'John slowly pushed the door, and as a result the door opened slowly.'
* 'John pushed the door slowly, and as a result the door opened (quickly).'

Also note that all the adverbs that modify V_2 (and v_{CAUSE} as well) in (49) are semantically change-of-state modifiers. These adverbs in Mandarin canonically modify inchoative predicates, and can modify simplex change-of-state predicates, as in (51).

(51) a. men manmande/xunsude/yixiazi   /mashang   **kai**-le.
door slowly   /quickly /all.of.a.sudden/immediately open-ASP
'The door opened slowly/quickly/all of a sudden/immediately.'

b. shuye yijing /manmande/yiyezhijian   **(bian)**   **huang**-le.
leaf   already/slowly   /over.a.single.night become yellow-ASP
'The leaves already/slowly/quickly/over a single night became yellow.'

c. bing yijing /manmande/xunsude/yiyezhijian   **hua**-le.
ice   already/slowly   /quickly /over.a.single.night melt-ASP
'The ice melted already/slowly/quickly/over a single night.'

I therefore argue that this adverbial modification pattern provides argument for the existence of the change-of-state head v_{BECOME} in the object-oriented V-V resultatives.

The second modification pattern is that adverbs like *you* 'again', *chayidian* 'almost', *zhongyu* 'finally', and *henkuai* 'very soon', when occurring in object-oriented V-V resultatives, can either modify both V_1 and V_2, or modify just V_2, as demonstrated in (52).

(52) a. John <u>you</u>   ba   zhuozi **zhuang-dao**-le.
     John again BA table hit-fall-ASP
     i. 'John knocked down the table again (He knocked it down before).'
     ii. 'John knocked down the table again (The table fell before).'

  b. John <u>chayidian</u> **tui-dao** wo.
     John almost   push-fall me
     i. '(John was angry at me and) he almost (came over and) pushed me down.'
     ii. 'John pushed me and I almost fell down.'

  c. John <u>henkuai</u>   **kan-dao**-le   na-ke   shu.
     John very.soon cut-fall-ASP that-CL tree
     i. '(I told John to cut down that tree and) he did so very soon.'
     ii. 'John chopped at that tree and in no time the tree fell.'

  d. John <u>zhongyu</u> **kan-dao**-le na-ke   shu.
     John finally   cut-fall-ASP that-CL tree
     i. 'John finally cut down that tree (after hesitating whether to do so for a long time).'
     ii. 'John finally cut down that tree (after cutting it for hours).'

Also note that the adverbs in (52), like those in (48) and (49), are all change-of-state modifiers, and can modify simplex change-of-state predicates, as shown in (53) and (54).

(53) na-ke   shu you /henkuai /zhongyu/chayidian **dao**-le.
     that-CL tree again/very.soon/finally /almost   fall-ASP
     'That tree /almost/fell/again/very soon/finally.'

(54) bing you /henkuai /zhongyu/chayidian **hua**-le.
     ice again/very.soon/finally /almost   melt-ASP
     'The ice (almost) melted again/very soon/finally.'

I argue that these examples provide further evidence for the existence of a v_{BECOME} head in the syntactic structure of object-oriented V-V resultatives. In (52), the (i) readings imply a CAUSE-BECOME event, while the (ii) readings indicate the existence of an independent BECOME subevent. Following von Stechow (1996), I assume that in these examples the adverbs in the restitutive readings modify the v_{BECOME} head. To summarize, based on the adverb modification properties presented above, I argue that a v_{BECOME} head is projected in the syntactic structure of object-oriented V-V resultatives.

Having provided the evidence for the v_{BECOME} head above, we now consider a situation involving the adverb *you* 'again', which might pose a challenge for this analysis. As presented object-oriented V-V resultatives containing the adverb *you* 'again' have two meanings: a repetitive meaning (52a-i), and a restitutive meaning (52a-ii). To further demonstrate the nature of *you* 'again' modification, we consider a scenario, in which a framed picture, originally hung on the wall in a straight and upright position, became slanted, and John adjusted the position of the picture so that it resumed its original upright position. As a description of this scenario, Mandarin speakers will accept the sentence in (55), which has a repetitive reading (55a) and a restitutive reading (55b).

(55) John <u>you</u> ba huakuang   **fu-zheng**-le.
    John again BA framed.picture adjust-be.upright-ASP
    a. 'John adjusted the picture to make it upright again (and he did this before).'
    b. 'The picture resumed its original upright position with John's adjustment.'

Note that, while the meaning of the repetitive reading (55a) is straightforward, the restitutive reading (55b) might be ambiguous. Arguably, (55b) can have two possible readings:

(i)   'The picture again **became** upright as a result of John's adjustment.'
(ii)   'The picture **was** upright again as a result of John's adjustment.'

In reading (ii), the adverb *you* 'again' modifies a v_{BE} head, not a v_{BECOME} head. So this reading, if indeed available, raises a problem for my analysis that a v_{BECOME} head, but not a v_{BE} head, is projected in object-oriented V-V resultatives. In this section, I demonstrate that while (55b) can invoke the reading (ii), the adverb *you* 'again' in Mandarin actually cannot modify a state, and I therefore argue that reading (ii) is not the direct interpretation of the syntactic structure. In Sect. 3.4.1.3, I will provide further evidence that the v_{BE} head is not projected in Mandarin V-V resultatives.

The adverb *you* 'again' cannot modify a stative predicates, as can be illustrated with the following examples. In Mandarin, the aspectual particle *zhe* indicates that a situation is enduring and continuing and it marks a state predicate, as illustrated in (56a). Note that, as shown in (56b), the adverb *you* 'again' cannot modify this stative predicate. More examples that illustrate this property of the adverb *you* 'again' in Mandarin are given in (57) and (58).

(56) a. men kai-zhe.   b. *men you   kai-zhe.
      door open-ASP   doo again open-ASP
      'The door is open.'   Intended meaning: 'The door is open again.'

(57) a. wo hen pang.   b. *wo you   hen pang.
      I   very fat   I   again very fat
      'I am very fat.'   Intended meaning: 'I am fat again.'

(58) a. wo xihuan kafei.   b. *wo you   xihuan kafei.
      I   like   coffee   I   again like   coffee
      'I like coffee.'   Intended meaning: 'I like coffee again.'

On the other hand, *you* 'again' can modify change-of-state predicates, as illustrated in the examples in (59) and (60).

(59) a. ta you   pang-(*le).
         he again fat-asp
         'He became fat again.'

   b. ni zenmo you e-(*le)?
      you how again hungery-asp
      'Why are you hungry again?'

(60) a. shuye you   bian   huang-le.
         leaf   again become yellow-ASP
         'The leaves became yellow again.'

   b. tade gebo you   duan-le.
      his arm again break-ASP
      'His arm broke again.'

   c. you jia   you   zhang-le.
      oil price again rise-ASP
      'The oil price rose again.'

The examples in (59) are of particular interest. In (59), *you* 'again' occurs with the adjectives *pang* 'fat' and *e* 'hungery', which might leave the impression that *you* 'again' can modify a state. However, note that in these examples, the aspect marker *le* is obligatory, and it has been agreed in the literature that aspect marker *le* makes the predicate a change-of-state predicate (e.g., Li & Thompson, 1981; Lin, 2004). These examples thus provide further support that the adverb *you* 'again' cannot modify state in Mandarin.[4]

Based on the data above, I argue that, in the example in (55), repeated in (61), the adverb *you* 'again' modifies a v_{BECOME} head, not a v_{BE} head. I propose that the reading 'The picture **was** upright again as a result of John's adjustment' is a pragmatic implication, rather than the (direct) interpretation of the syntactic structure of the sentence.

(61) John <u>you</u> ba   huakuang   **fu-zheng**-le.
     John again BA framed.picture adjust-be.upright-ASP
     a. 'John adjusted the picture to make it upright again (and he did this before).'
     b. 'The picture resumed its original upright position with John's adjustment.'

To summarize, in this section, I have argued that, in Mandarin object-oriented resultatives, a $v_{BECOME}P$ expressing the change-of-state meaning is projected. In the next section, I show that the $v_{BE}P$, which Lin (2004) claims to exist in Mandarin V-V resultatives, is actually not present.

3.4.1.3   The Absence of $v_{BE}P$

If we hypothesize that a $v_{BE}P$ is projected in the syntactic structure of object-oriented resultatives, we predict that adverbs that modify states should be able to occur in causatives. However, this is not the case. In the first place, none of the adverbs that

---

[4]Zhang points out this interesting point to me (personal communication).

modify V_2 in causatives can modify a simplex stative predicate in Mandarin, as demonstrated in (62).

(62) a. John chayidian/yijing /manmande/xunsude/yixiazi kaishi **xihuan** na-ben shu-le.
　　　John almost　　/already/slowly　　/quickly /suddenly begin like　　that-CL book-ASP
　　　'John almost/ already/slowly/quickly/suddenly began to like that book.'

　　b. John *{chayidian/yijing /manmande/xunsude/yixiazi} **xihuan** na-ben shu.
　　　John almost　　/already/ slowly　/quickly /suddenly like　　that-CL book

On the other hand, adverbs that modify a simplex stative predicate cannot occur in object-oriented V-V resultatives. We take the adverb *hen* 'very' as an example. In Mandarin, the adverb *hen* 'very' modifies states. Notably, this adverb cannot occur in V-V resultatives to modify V_2, as shown in (63)–(65).

(63) a. shuye (biancheng) hen **huang**-le.
　　　leaf　become　　very yellow-ASP
　　　'The leaves had become deep yellow in colour.'

　　b. qiufeng　(*hen) **chui-huang**-le　　shuye.
　　　fall.wind　very blow-yellow-ASP leaf
　　　Intended meaning: 'The wind of the fall blew the leaves into a deep yellow colour.'

(64) a. na-kuai tie-pian　　hen **bao**.
　　　that-CL metal-plate very be.thin
　　　'That piece of metal plate is very thin.'

　　b. John (*hen) **mo-bao**-le　　na-kuai tie-pian.
　　　John　very rub-be.thin-ASP that-CL metal-plate
　　　Intended meaning: 'John rubbed that metal plate so that it was very thin.'

(65) a. yifu　yijing hen **gan**-le.
　　　clothes already very be.dry-ASP
　　　'The clothes are already very dry.'

　　b. taiyang (*hen) **shai-gan**-le　　yifu.
　　　sun　　very air-be.dry-ASP clothes
　　　Intended meaning: 'The sun aired the clothes to a very dry state.'

I argue that this adverbial modification property indicates that no $v_{BE}P$ is projected in the syntactic structure of object-oriented resultatives.

3.4.1.4 An Interim Summary

In Sect. 3.4, I have argued that the basic syntactic structure of Mandarin object-oriented V-V resultatives is a double-layered vP structure, as shown in (66) below. Note that essentially this is the structure that various authors have proposed for direct causatives (Hale & Keyser, 1993; Harley, 2008, 2017; Pylkkänen, 2008; Travis, 2010).

(66)

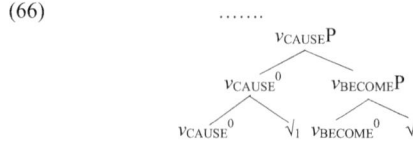

We now consider how the two verb roots integrate into the basic syntactic structure for object-oriented V-V resultatives. It has been proposed in the literature that verbs fall into two categories, manner and result, and these ontological categories determine how verb meaning gets associated with event structure (Alexiadou, Anagnostopoulou, & Schäfer, 2015; Embick, 2004; Harley, 2005; Rappaport Hovav & Levin, 1998). According to these authors, manner roots specify a manner in which an action is carried out; syntactically, manner roots adjoin to the v head, as illustrated in (67a). Result roots, on the other hand, specify a result state; in terms of syntactic structure, the result root phrases are complements of v, as in (67b).

(67) a. Manner roots as modifiers of v b. Result roots as complements of v

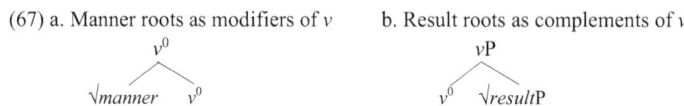

Extending this analysis to the Mandarin object-oriented V-V resultatives, I propose that the first verbal root $\sqrt{_1}$ adjoins to the v_{CAUSE} head. Semantically, $\sqrt{_1}$ modifies the event represented by the v_{CAUSE} head, indicating the manner of the causation. With regard to the relation between the v_{BECOME} head and $\sqrt{_2}$, I propose that the $\sqrt{_2}P$ merges with the v_{BECOME} head as its complement, denoting what state the theme object comes into as a result of the CAUSE event.

As for the structural position of the arguments, following Kratzer (1996), I assume that, the external argument is introduced by a functional head Voice (this will be the focus of the next chapter). On the other hand, following a number of proposals in the literature (Hale & Keyser, 1993; Harley, 2011; Levin & Rappaport Hovav, 1995; Travis, 2010), I assume that, the structural position for the internal theme argument of the change-of-state predicate (V_2) is the specifier of the $v_{BECOME}P$. Taking the Mandarin V-V resultatives in (68) as an example, the proposed syntactic structure is as in (69). In (69a, b), the heads realized by $\sqrt{_2}$ raise to the position following the head realized with $\sqrt{_2}$, forming the surface V-V compounds.

(68) a. John **kan-dao**-le shu.   b. John **ku-shi**-le   maojin.
     John cut-fall-ASP tree   John cry-be.wet-ASP towel
     'John cut down that tree.'   'John cried and got the towel wet.'

(69) a.   b.

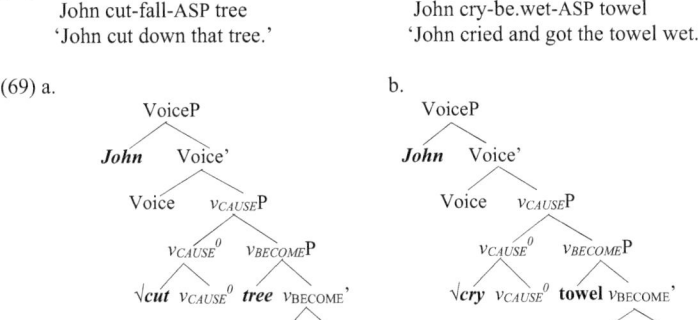

As I indicated in (36), in these syntactic structures, the position for the adverbs is the specifier of the vP. To be more specific, when the adverbs modify v_{CAUSE} or both v_{CAUSE} and v_{BECOME}, their position is in the specifier of the v_{CAUSE}P; when they modify just v_{BECOME}, their position is the specifier of the v_{BECOME}P.

In the Sect. 3.4.2, I consider the syntactic structure of subject-oriented V-V resultatives. I will argue that, in this construction, only a v_{BECOME} head is projected—v_{CAUSE} and v_{BE} are absent. That is, subject-oriented V-V resultatives are unaccusative predicates.

3.4.2 The Syntactic Structure of Subject-Oriented V-V Resultatives

The other type of V-V resultatives in Mandarin, the subject-oriented V-V resultatives, is exemplified in (70).

(70) a. John **zou-lei**-le.
    John walk-be.tired-ASP
    'John got tired from walking.'

  b. John **he-zui**-le.
    John drink-be.drunk-ASP
    'John got drunk from drinking.'

One basic difference between object-oriented and subject-oriented V-V resultatives is that, in subject-oriented resultatives, both V_1 and V_2 are predicated of the subject: V_1 denotes the event that the subject has initiated, and V_2, the state that this subject comes into as a result of the V_1 event. In other words, while object-oriented resultatives express the meaning that the subject, in the manner of V_1, causes the theme object to come into the V_2 state, the subject-oriented resultatives convey the meaning that the subject (himself) becomes, or experiences, the V_2 state as the result of conducting the V_1 activity.

Previous analyses generally analyze object-oriented resultatives and subject-oriented resultatives as having the same syntactic structure (e.g., Cheng & Huang, 1994; Lin, 2004; Wang, 2010). In this section, I show that subject-oriented resultatives demonstrate different adverbial modification properties from object-oriented resultatives, and based on this, I argue that they have different syntactic structures. Specifically, I propose that subject-oriented V-V resultatives have the basic syntactic structure shown in (71). In this structure, only a $v_{\text{BECOME}}P$ is projected; the root of V_1 is a modifier of the head v_{BECOME}, and this head takes the root of V_2 as its complement. On this analysis, subject-oriented V-V resultatives in Mandarin actually have the syntactic structure of unaccusative inchoative predicates.

(71)

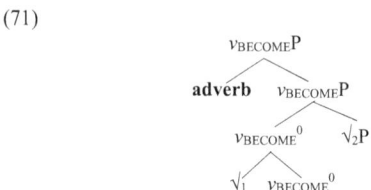

In what follows, I present the adverbial modification properties of subject-oriented resultatives, and demonstrate how these properties provide evidence for the structure in (71).

3.4.2.1   Adverbial Modification Properties of Subject-Oriented V-V Resultatives

Generally speaking, subject-oriented resultatives demonstrate the following three adverbial modification properties. First, V_1 can hardly be modified by any adverbs; secondly, time adverbs such as *yijing* 'already', *mashang* 'immediately', *manmande* 'slowly', and adverbs like *you* 'again', *zhongyu* 'finally', and *chayidian* 'almost', can modify V_2; thirdly, state modifiers are not allowed. I demonstrate these three properties in what follows.

V_1: *Unavailable for Adverbial Modification*

First, as in object-oriented resultatives, adverbs that modify an activity, i.e. v_{DO} modifiers, are not able to modify V_1 in subject-oriented resultatives, as shown in the following examples.

(72) a. John zhengzai <u>kuai</u> /<u>man</u> **zou**.
  John PROG quickly/slowly walk.
  'John is walking quickly/slowly.'

  b. John (*kuai /*man) **zou-lei**-le.
  John quickly/ slowly walk-be.tired-ASP
  Intended meaning: 'John got tired by walking quickly/slowly.'

(73) a. John zhengzai <u>dashengde</u> **ku**.
  John PROG loudly cry
  'John is crying loudly.'

  b. John (*<u>dashengde</u>) **ku-xing**-le.
  John loudly cry-wake-ASP
  Intended meaning: 'John cried loudly and as a result he woke.'

(74) a. John <u>butingde</u> **ting** na-shou ge.
  John repeatedly listen that-CL song
  'John listened to that song repeatedly.'

  b. John (*<u>butingde</u>) **ting-ni**-le na-shou ge.
  John repeatedly listen-be.bored-ASP that-CL song
  Intended meaning: 'John got bored of that song after listening to it repeatedly.'

Based on this adverbial modification property, I argue that the head v_{DO} is not projected in subject-oriented V-V resultatives.

Secondly, V_1 in subject-oriented resultatives cannot be modified by manner adverbs or agentive adverbs. In contrast, as demonstrated in Sect. 3.4.1.1, V_1 in object-oriented resultatives can be modified by (certain) manner adverbs and agentive adverbs. This is shown in (75), repeated from (30a) and (32b). I have argued that these adverbs actually modify the v_{CAUSE} head.

(75) Object-oriented resultatives

  a. John <u>yijiao</u> **ti-kai**-le men.
  John one.kick kick-open-ASP door
  'John kicked the door open with (just) one kick.'

  b. John <u>yonglide</u> /shengqide **tui-kai** na-shan men.
  John forcefully/angrily push-open that-CL door
  'John pushed that door forcefully/angrily and got it open.'

A conspicuous difference between subject-oriented resultatives and object-oriented resultatives is that V_1 of subject-oriented resultatives cannot be modified by these adverbs, as illustrated in (76). We consider (76a) first. Suppose John was kicking something hard, and after only one kick, he felt pain in his foot. This situation cannot be expressed with (76a). That is, manner adverbs cannot modify V_1 in subject-oriented resultatives. (76b) indicates that V_1 cannot be modified by agentive adverbs neither.

(76) a. John (*yijiao)   **ti-teng**-le.
　　　 John　 one.kick kick-feel.pain-ASP
　　　 Intended meaning: 'John felt pain in his foot after only one kick.'

　　 b. John (*yonglide /shengqide) **zou-lei**-le.
　　　 John　 forcefully/angrily　 walk-be.tired-ASP
　　　 Intended meaning: 'John walked forcefully/angrily, and as a result he got tired.'

I argued above that, all the apparent V_1 modifiers in object-oriented V-V resultatives are actually v_{CAUSE} modifiers. Thus whether these adverbs can occur or not reflects the presence/absence of the v_{CAUSE} head. Following this line of reasoning, I argue that the v_{CAUSE} head is not projected in subject-oriented V-V resultatives.

Adverbial Modification of V_2

The second main adverbial modification property of subject-oriented resultatives, as noted earlier, is that adverbs that indicate a meaning associated with time, such as *yijing* 'already', *mashang* 'immediately', *like* 'immediately', *manmande* 'slowly', *xunshu* 'quickly', and adverbs like *you* 'again', *zhongyu* 'finally', and *chayidian* 'almost', can modify V_2. I demonstrate this property by contrasting subject-oriented and object-oriented V-V resultatives. I argue that it provides evidence for the existence of the v_{BECOME} head in both types of resultatives, and that it also provides further evidence for the lack of the v_{CAUSE} head in subject-oriented resultatives.

On the one hand, as with object-oriented resultatives, time adverbs and adverbs like *you* 'again', *zhongyu* 'finally', and *chayidian* 'almost', can occur in subject-oriented resultatives to modify V_2. This is demonstrated in (77) and (78).

(77) a. John yixiazi　　　 **ku-xing**-le.
　　　 John all.of.a.sudden cry-wake-ASP
　　　 'John cried and woke all of a sudden.'

　　 b. John yijing /manmande　　　 **zou-lei**-le.
　　　 John already/slowly.gradually walk-be.tired-ASP
　　　 'John got tired already/soon/gradually.'

(78) a. John you /chayidian **he-zui**-le.
　　　 John again/almost　 drink-be.drunk-ASP
　　　 'John got drunk from drinking again/John almost got drunk from drinking.'

　　 b. John henkuai　 /zhongyu **chi-bao**-le.
　　　 John very.soon/finally　 eat-be.full-ASP
　　　 'Very soon/finally, John got full (from eating).'

Since these adverbs are change-of-state modifiers, as I have demonstrated in Sect. 3.4.1, I conclude that the v_{BECOME} head is projected in subject-oriented resultatives.

On the other hand, subject-oriented resultatives demonstrate a crucial difference from object-oriented resultatives in adverbial modification by time adverbs and adverbs like *you* 'again', *zhongyu* 'finally', and *chayidian* 'almost'. We consider time adverbs first. Recall that, when time adverbs occur in object-oriented resultatives, they modify both v_{CAUSE} and v_{BECOME}. As demonstrated in (79), when the adverb *manmande* 'slowly' modifies the object-oriented resultative *tui-kai* 'push-open', it modifies both the pushing action and the way that the door becomes open. I have argued for the existence of two separate heads in object-oriented resultatives, v_{CAUSE} and v_{BECOME}. However, when such adverbs occur in subject-oriented resultatives, they modify just V_2, not V_1. As (80) demonstrates, when *manmande* 'slowly' modifies the subject-oriented resultative *zou-lei* 'walk-be tired', this sentence does not mean 'John walked slowly and as a result he got tired'—it only means 'Gradually, John got tired from walking.' This property provides further evidence for the lack of v_{CAUSE} in subject-oriented resultatives.

(79) John <u>manmande</u> **tui-kai**-le   men.
    John slowly   push-open-ASP door
    i. *'John pushed the door slowly, and as a result the door opened (quickly).'
    ii. √'John slowly pushed the door, and as a result the door opened slowly.'

(80) John <u>manmande</u> **zou-lei**-le.
    John slowly   walk-be.tired-ASP
    i. *'John walked slowly and as a result he got tired.'
    ii. √'Gradually, John got tired from walking.'

Next we consider adverbs like *you* 'again', *zhongyu* 'finally', and *chayidian* 'almost'. As demonstrated in Sect. 3.4.1, when these adverbs occur in object-oriented resultatives, the sentences have two readings, as illustrated in (81), repeated from (53). In contrast, when these adverbs occur in subject-oriented resultatives, these sentences have only one reading, in which the adverbs modify just V_2, but not V_1. The examples in (82) illustrate this.

(81) Object-oriented resultatives

    a. John <u>you</u>   ba   zhuozi **zhuang-dao**-le.
    John again BA table   hit-fall-ASP
    i. 'John knocked down the table again (He knocked it down before).'
    ii. 'John knocked down the table again (The table fell before).'

    b. John <u>chayidian</u> **tui-dao** wo.
    John almost   push-fall me
    i. '(John was angry at me and) he almost (came over and) pushed me down.'
    ii. 'John pushed me and I almost fell down.'

    c. John <u>henkuai</u>   **kan-dao**-le na-ke   shu.
    John very.soon cut-fall-ASP that-CL tree
    i. '(I told John to cut down that tree and) he did so very soon.'
    ii. 'John chopped at that tree and in no time the tree fell.'

    d. John <u>zhongyu</u> **kan-dao**-le na-ke   shu.
    John finally   cut-fall-ASP that-CL tree
    i. 'John finally cut down that tree (after hesitating whether to do so for a long time).'
    ii. 'John finally cut down that tree (after cutting it for hours).'

(82) Subject-oriented resultatives

    a. John <u>chayidian</u> **he-zui**-le.
    John almost   drink-be.drunk-ASP
    i. *'John almost took a drink, with the possible result or goal of getting drunk.'
    ii. √ 'John drank and nearly/almost got drunk.'

    b. John <u>henkuai</u>   **he-zui**-le.
    John very.soon drink-be.drunk-ASP
    i. *'(I told John to drink until he was drunk,) he did so very soon.'
    ii. √ 'John got drunk very soon through drinking.'

    c. John <u>zhongyu</u> **chi-bao**-le.
    John finally   eat-be.full-ASP
    i. *'Finally, John had a chance to eat, and got full.'
    ii. √'John finally got full (after eating much food).'

For object-oriented resultatives, I argued that the two readings generated by the modification of this group of adverbs indicate two separate heads, v_{CAUSE} and v_{BECOME}, in the syntactic structure of these constructions. Following this line of reasoning, I conclude that the single reading for subject-oriented resultatives indicates that there is just a single vP in these constructions, which is v_{BECOME}P.

The Impossibility of State-Modifying Adverbs

The third property of subject-oriented resultatives is that no state-modifying adverbs are possible in these constructions, as is shown in (83) and (84). I argue that this is because there is no v_{BE} head in the syntactic structure of these constructions.

(83) a. John ganjue <u>hen</u> **lei**.
     John feel   very be.tired
     'John felt very tired.'

    b. John (*<u>hen</u>) **zou-lei**-le.   /John **zou** (*<u>hen</u>) **lei**-le.
      John   very walk-be.tired-ASP /John walk very be.tired-ASP
      Intended meaning: 'John got very tired from walking.'

(84) a. John <u>hen</u> **fan**   na-shou ge.
     John very be.sick that-CL song
     'John is very sick of that song.'

    b. *John <u>hen</u> **ting-fan**-le   na-shou ge.
     John very listen-be.sick-ASP that-CL song
     Intended meaning: 'John is very sick of that song due to (too much) listening.'

Based on the adverbial modification properties presented above, I argue that the syntactic structure of subject-oriented V-V resultatives contains only one vP headed by v_{BECOME}. To demonstrate this analysis, I propose that subject-oriented V-V resultatives such as (85a) have the syntactic structure in (85b).

(85) a. John **zou-lei**-le.
     John walk-be.tired-ASP
     'John got tired from walking.'

    b.

In the next section, I consider a special case of subject-oriented resultatives, that is, subject-oriented resultatives that contain a surface object. In particular, I will examine the introduction of this surface object.

3.4.2.2   Subject-Oriented V-V Resultatives with Surface Object

As we have seen, the canonical form of subject-oriented resultatives is DP$_{subject}$ V$_1$ + V$_2$. In some subject-oriented V-V resultatives, however, as demonstrated in (86), the theme object of a transitive V$_1$ can appear after V$_2$ (and the aspectual marker if present).

(86) John **chi-bao**   fan-le.
     John eat-be.full meal-ASP
     'John got full by eating his meal.'

In (86), *fan* 'meal' is the theme argument of V$_1$ *chi* 'eat', and it has no semantic relation to V$_2$ *bao* 'be full', which is predicated of the subject *John*. Also, this NP possesses none of the properties of canonical theme objects, as I will demonstrate below. I will call this NP *surface object*. Here we may also consider another example, in (87), which is much discussed in the literature (Cheng & Huang, 1994; Han, 2017; Y. Li, 1990; Lin, 2004). The sentence in (87) has two readings: an object-oriented reading (87a), and a subject-oriented reading (87b). That is, like (86), (87b) is the reading of a subject-oriented resultative containing a surface object.

(87) John **qi-lei**-le   ma-le.
  John ride-be.tired-ASP horse-ASP
  a. Object-oriented reading: 'The horse got tired because of John's riding.'
  b. Subject-oriented reading: 'John got tired from riding the horse.'

Subject-oriented resultatives with surface objects demonstrate exactly the same adverbial modification properties as those without a surface object. Based on this, I assume that this special case has the same basic syntactic structure as the canonical ones that do not contain a surface object.

I now consider the syntactic character of the surface object. One conspicuous property of the surface objects in (86) and (87b) is that they are not ordinary objects of the V-V resultatives, as they possess no properties of canonical objects. I demonstrate this below.

In the first place, a surface object is normally not a fully referential argument (e.g., Huang, 2006; Lin, 2004), as in (88).

(88) a. John **chi-bao**-le   (*san-dun) fan.
   John eat-be.full-ASP (three-CL) meal
   Intended meaning: 'John got full after eating meals.'

   b. John **he-zui**-le   (*liang-ping) jiu.
    John drink-be.drunk-ASP (two-bottle) wine
    Intended meaning: 'John got drunk after drinking two bottles of wine.'

In (88a, b) the object *fan* 'meal' and *jiu* 'wine' are bare NPs, and they do not denote any specific meal or wine that has been eaten or drunk. Likewise, in (87b), the bare NP *ma* 'horse' does not denote any particular horse—rather, it simply helps to denote a horse-riding activity. If we replace the bare NP *ma* 'horse' with a full DP such as *san-pi ma* 'three horses', as shown in (89), the subject-oriented reading is unavailable; the sentence only has an object-oriented reading (Han, 2017; Huang, 2006).[5]

(89) John **qi-lei**-le   san-pi   ma.
  John ride-be.tired-ASP three-CL horse
  √ Object-oriented reading: 'Three horses got tired because of John's riding.'
  * Subject-oriented reading: 'John got tired from riding three horses.'

---

[5]Zhang (personal communication) notes that the surface object in some subject-oriented V-V resultatives does seem to be referential, as shown in (i).

 (i) John **chuan-ni**-le na-shuang xiezi.
 John wear-be.sick-asp that-CL shoe.
 'John gets sick of that pair of shoes after wearing them (too much).'.

 In my judgement, there seems to be a thematic relation between the object 'that pair of shoes' and V_2 'be sick of'. That is, this class of examples may be object-oriented V-V resultatives rather than subject-oriented V-V resultatives. I leave a further exploration of this for future work.

Second, subject-oriented resultatives with surface objects do not passivize—a passive counterpart to the sentence cannot be constructed by moving the surface object to the left edge of the sentence, and recasting the agent as a preverbal element following *BEI*, as in (90).

(90) a. *fan bei John **chi-bao**-le.
     meal BEI John eat-be.full-ASP

   b. *jiu bei John **he-zui**-le.
     wine BEI John drink-be.drunk-ASP

Note that, in contrast with subject-oriented V-V resultatives with a surface object, object-oriented V-V resultatives have corresponding passive constructions, as is illustrated in (91).

(91) a. John **ti-kai**-le   men.
     John kick-open-ASP door
     'John kicked the door open.'

   b. men bei (John) **ti-kai**-le.
     tree BEI (John) kick-open-ASP
     'The door was kicked open (by John).'

A third character of subject-oriented V-V resultatives containing a surface object is that they cannot convert to the *BA*-construction. The basic word order in Mandarin is SVO (Li & Thompson, 1981). However, a transitive carrying a canonical object, like the one in (92a), can usually convert to the *BA*-construction, in which the object appears in the position immediately preceding the verb and following the morpheme *ba* (92b). Generally speaking, the original sentence and its corresponding *BA*-construction have the same meaning.

(92) a. John chi-le   nage pingguo.
     John eat-ASP that apple
     'John ate that apple.'

   b. John ba   nage pingguo chi-le.
     John BA that apple   eat-ASP
     'John ate that apple.'

The *BA*-construction demonstrates complex properties and has received much discussion in the literature (Ding, 2001; F. Liu, 1997; Sybesma, 1999; Zou, 1993; Ziegeler, 2000; among many others). While some aspects of the *BA*-construction are still controversial, it is generally agreed that semantically, the *BA*-construction indicates high transitivity, and syntactically the morpheme *ba* is a Case-assigning head, which assigns the structural object Case to the NP that immediately following it, the so-termed *ba-object* (Huang, Y. Li, & Y.-H. Li, 2009; Y. Li, 1990; Sun, 1996; Zou, 1993). Due to this property, the possibility of converting to the *BA*-construction has been identified as a canonical object property of a postverbal DP.

Note that subject-oriented V-V resultatives with surface objects cannot convert to the *BA*-construction, as shown in (93) and (94).

(93) a. John **chi-bao**-le   fan.
       John eat-be.full-ASP meal
       'John got full from eating his meal.'

   b. *John ba   fan **chi-bao**-le.
       John BA meal eat-full-ASP

(94) a. John **he-zui**-le   jiu.
       John drink-be.drunk-ASP wine
       Intended meaning: 'John got drunk from drinking wine.'

   b. *John ba jiu **he-zui**-le.
       John BA wine drink-be.drunk-ASP

Again, contrasting with subject-oriented V-V resultatives with surface objects, object-oriented V-V resultatives normally have corresponding *BA*-constructions, as shown in (95).

(95) a. John **ti-kai**-le   men.
       John kick-open-ASP door
       'John kicked the door open.'

   b. John ba men **ti-kai**-le.
       John BA door kick-open-ASP
       'John kicked the door open.'

Given these properties, I conclude that these surface objects are not the structural objects of subject-oriented V-V resultatives—that is to say, they are not thematically licensed in the specifier of v_{BECOME}P. Following Levin (1999) and Lin (2004), I propose that the surface object is thematically licensed by (the semantics of) the verbal root, specifically, the root $\sqrt{}_1$.

In an event-structure approach to the introduction of objects, Levin (1999) proposes that the object of a transitive verb can be thematically licensed in two different manners: by the event template, or by the verb root (*constant* in Levin's terms). Based on the different properties of their objects, Levin divides transitive verbs into two groups: transitive verbs that semantically fit the mould of an agent acting on, and causing an effect on a patient, which Levin terms *core transitive verbs* (CTV), and transitive verbs that do not fit this semantic profile, which Levin calls *non-core transitive verbs* (NCTV). On the other hand, Levin assumes two types of event templates: those expressing a complex (causative) event structure, as shown in (96a), and those expressing a simple event structure, as in (96b). The complex event template specifies two event participants (x and y), and thereby structurally introduces both the subject and the theme object; a simple event template, in contrast, specifies one event participant (x in the template), and can introduce only one argument, the subject.

(96) a. [[**x** ACT<*MANNER*>]] CAUSE [BECOME [**y**<STATE>]]]
    b. [**x** ACT<*MANNER*>]

Levin proposes that CTVs have a complex event structure, while NCTVs have a simple event structure. She argues that, for CTVs, their subjects and objects are introduced by the event template; for NCTVs, in contrast, their objects are not structurally introduced by the event template, but by the core meaning of the verb—that is, by the verbal root.

Similarly, Lin (2004) proposes that, in some cases, an activity verbal root can idiosyncratically introduce a DP, thus forming a transitive sentence. Lin proposes that, in the sentence in (97a), the DP *the marathon* is thematically introduced by the root $\sqrt{run}$, rather than structurally introduced by the v_{DO}P, as demonstrated in (97b).

(97) a. John ran the marathon.

b.

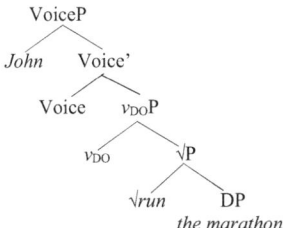

Moreover, Lin proposes that the surface object in a Mandarin subject-oriented V-V resultative is introduced by the root of V_1.

Following Levin (1999) and Lin (2004), I propose that the surface object in subject-oriented resultatives is introduced by $\sqrt{1}$, as illustrated in (98).

(98) a. John **chi-bao**-le   fan.
     John   eat-be.full-ASP   meal
     'John got full from eating his meal.'

b.

v_{BECOME}P
v_{BECOME}^0 $\sqrt{be\ full}$
v_{BECOME}^0 $\sqrt{}$P
$\sqrt{eat^0}$ meal

3.5 Conclusion

In this chapter, I have conducted an event-mapping analysis of the syntactic structure of V-V resultatives in Mandarin. By referring to, and arguing against, Lin's isomorphic analysis, I argued that the mapping between semantic event structure and syntactic argument structure is not implemented through a system in which each semantic subevent is realized and represented by a corresponding vP. Based on adverbial modification properties, I have shown that object-oriented and subject-oriented V-V resultatives in Mandarin have different structures, despite their similar surface form and resultative meanings. For object-oriented resultatives, their syntactic structure is the canonical v_{CAUSE}-v_{BECOME} structure for direct causatives proposed in the literature; as for subject-oriented resultatives, they are actually unaccusative predicates.

In the next chapter, I focus on subject properties and alternation properties of the two types of V-V resultatives. I will show that the subject of object-oriented resultatives is an external argument, while it is a derived subject in subject-oriented resultatives. I thus provide further support for the analysis that the two types of resultatives have different structures. Then, based on this 'two-structure' analysis, I will propose a new system to categorize the alternative uses of resultatives and to account for relevant alternation properties.

References

Alexiadou, A., Anagnostopoulou, E., & Schäfer, F. (2015). *External arguments in transitivity alternations: A layering approach.* Oxford: Oxford University Press.

Baker, M. (1988). *Incorporation: A theory of grammatical function changing.* Chicago: University of Chicago Press.

Bonami, O., Godard, D., & Manhe, B. (2004). Adverb classification. In F. Corblin, & H. de Swart (Eds.), *Handbook of French semantics* (pp. 143–184). Center for the Study of Language and Information.

Borer, H. (2005). *Structuring sense: In name only* (Vol. 1). Oxford: Oxford University Press.

Bowers, J. (1993). The syntax of predication. *Linguistic Inquiry, 24,* 591–656.

Bowers, J. (1997). A binary analysis of resultatives. *Texas Linguistics Forum, 38,* 43–58.

Bowers, J. (2000). Predication. In M. Baltin, & C. Collins (Eds.), *The handbook of contemporary syntactic theory* (pp. 299–333). Blackwell.

Bresnan, J. (Ed.). (1982). *The mental representation of grammatical relations.* Cambridge, MA: MIT Press.

Carter, R. (1976). Some constraints on possible words. *Semantikos, 1,* 27–66.

Cheng, L. & Huang, C.-T. (1994). On the argument structure of resultative compounds. In Y. Chen, J. Ovid, & L. Tzeng (Eds.), *In Honour of William S.-Y. Wang: Interdisciplinary studies in language and language change* (pp. 187–221). Taiwan: Pyramid.

Chomsky, N. (1995). *Minimalist program.* Cambridge MA.: MIT Press.

Collins, C. (1997). Argument sharing in serial verb constructions. *Linguistic Inquiry, 28,* 461–497.

Collins, C. (2005). A smuggling approach to raising in English. *Linguistic Inquiry, 36*(2), 289–298.

Ding, P. (2001). Semantic change versus categorical change: A study of the development of BA in Mandarin. *Journal of Chinese Linguistics, 29*(1), 102–128.

Di Sciullo, A., & Williams, E. (1987). *On the definition of word.* Cambridge, MA.: MIT Press.

Dowty, D. (1979). *Word meaning and montague grammar.* Dordrecht: Reidel.

Embick, D. (2004). On the structure of resultative participles in English. *Linguistic Inquiry, 35,* 355–392.

Fillmore, C. (1968). The case for case. In E. Bach & R. Harms (Eds.), *Universals in linguistic theory* (pp. 1–90). New York: Rinehart & Winston.

Grimshaw, J. (1990). *Argument structure.* Cambridge, MA: MIT Press.

Hale, K., & Keyser, S. (1993). On argument structure and the lexical expression of syntactic relations. In K. Hale & S. Keyser (Eds.), *The view from building 20* (pp. 53–109). Cambridge, MA.: MIT Press.

Halle, M., & Marantz, A. (1993). Distributed Morphology and the pieces of inflection. In K. Hale, & S. Keyser (Eds.), *The view from building* (Vol. 20, pp. 111–176). Cambridge, MA.: MIT Press.

Han, P. (2017). A force-theoretic approach to Mandarin single-clause resultative constructions. In *Proceedings of the Annual Conference of the Canadian Linguistic Association* (pp 1–13).

Harley, H. (2005). How do verbs get their names? Denominal verbs, manner incorporation, and the ontology of verb roots in English. In N. Erteschik-Shir, & T. Rapoport (Eds.), *The syntax of aspect. Deriving thematic and aspectual interpretation* (pp. 42–64). Oxford: Oxford University Press.

Harley, H. (2008). On the causative construction. In S. Miyagawa & M. Saito (Eds.), *Handbook of Japanese linguistics* (pp. 20–53). Oxford: Oxford University Press.

Harley, H. (2011). Affixation and the Mirror Principle. In R. Folli & C. Ullbricht (Eds.), *Interfaces in linguistics* (pp. 166–186). Oxford: Oxford University Press.

Harley, H. (2017). The "bundling" hypothesis and the disparate functions of little v. In R. D'Alessandro, I. Franco, & A. Gallego (Eds.), *The verbal domain* (pp. 3–28). Oxford: Oxford University Press.

Her, O. (2007). Argument-function mismatches in Mandarin Resultatives: A lexical mapping account. *Lingua, 117,* 221–246.

Hoekstra, T. (1988). Small clause results. *Lingua, 74,* 101–139.

Hornstein, N., & Lightfoot, D. (1987). Predication and PRO. *Language, 63,* 23–52.

Huang, C.-T. (1992). Complex predicates in control. In R. Larson, U. Lahiri, S. Iatridou, & J. Higginbotham (Eds.), *Control and grammar* (pp. 109–147). Dordrecht: Kluwer.

Huang, C.-T. (2006). Resultatives and unaccusatives: A parametric view. *Bulletin of the Chinese Linguistic Society of Japan, 253,* 1–43.

Huang, C.-T., Li, A., & Li. Y. (2009). *The syntax of Chinese.* Cambridge: Cambridge, UK: University Press.

Jackendoff, R. (1972). *Semantic interpretation in generative grammar.* Cambridge, MA.: MIT Press.

Jackendoff, R. (1975). Morphological and semantic regularities in the lexicon. *Language, 51,* 639–671.

Kratzer, A. (1996). Severing the external argument from its verb. In J. Rooryck & L. Zaring (Eds.), *Phrase structure and the lexicon* (pp. 109–137). Dordrecht: Kluwer.

Kyle, J., & Beck, S. (2004). Double objects again. *Linguistic Inquiry, 35*(1), 97–123.

Larson, R. (1988). On the double object construction. *Linguistic Inquiry, 19,* 335–391.

Levin, B. (1999). Objecthood: An event structure perspective. In *Proceedings of the 35th Annual Meeting of the Chicago Linguistics Society* (pp. 223–247).

Levin, B., & Rappaport Hovav, M. (1995). *Unaccusativity: At the syntax-lexical semantics interface.* Cambridge, MA.: MIT Press.

Li, Y. (1990). On V-V compounds in Chinese. *Natural Language & Linguistic Theory, 8,* 177–207.

Li, Y. (1993). Structural head and aspectuality. *Language, 69,* 480–504.

Li, Y. (2005). X^0: A theory of the morphology-syntax interface: A theory of the morphology-syntax interface. Cambridge, MA: MIT Press.

Lin, J. (2004). *Event structure and the encoding of arguments: The syntax of the Mandarin and English verb phrase.* Doctoral dissertation. Massachusetts Institute of Technology.

Li, C., & Thompson, S. (1981). *Mandarin Chinese: A functional reference grammar.* Berkeley: University of California Press.

Liu, F. (1997). An aspectual analysis of *ba*. *Journal of East Asian Linguistics, 6*(1), 51–99.

Liu, H. (2004). *Complex predicates in Mandarin Chinese: Three types of Bu-Yu structures.* Doctoral dissertation. University of California.

Marantz, A. (1997). No escape from syntax: Don't try morphological analysis in the privacy of your own lexicon. In A. Dimitriadis, & L. Siegel (Eds.), *University of Pennsylvania Working Papers in Linguistics. Proceedings of the 21st Annual Penn Linguistics Colloquium* (Vol. 4, pp. 201–225).

Marantz, A. (2013). Verbal argument structure: Events and participants. *Lingua, 130,* 152–168.

McCawley, J. (1968). Lexical insertion in a transformational grammar without deep structure. In B. Darden, C. Bailey, & A. Davison (Eds.), *Papers from the Fourth Meeting of the Chicago Linguistic Society* (pp. 71–80). Chicago: University of Chicago.

Mulder, R. (1992). *The aspectual aspectual nature of syntactic complementation.* Doctoral dissertation. University of Leiden.

Nishiyama, K. (1998). V-V compounds as serialization. *Journal of East Asian Linguistics, 7,* 175–217.

Perlmutter, D. (1988). The split morphology hypothesis: Evidence from Yiddish. In M. Hammond & M. Noonan (Eds.), *Theoretical morphology* (pp. 79–99). San Diego: Academic Press Inc.

Pustejovsky, J. (1995). *The generative lexicon.* Cambridge, MA: MIT Press.

Pylkkänen, L. (2008). *Introducing arguments.* Cambridge, MA: MIT Press.

Ramchand, G. (2008). *Verb meaning and the lexicon: A first-phase syntax.* Cambridge: Cambridge University Press.

Rappaport Hovav, M., & Levin, B. (1998). Building verb meanings. In M. Butt & W. Geuder (Eds.), *The projection of arguments* (pp. 97–134). Stanford: CSLI Publications.

Ritter, E., & Rosen, S. (2000). Event structure and ergativity. In C. Tenny & J. Pustejovsky (Eds.), *Events as grammatical objects: The converging perspectives of lexical semantics and syntax* (pp. 187–238). Stanford: CSLI Publications.

Schäfer, F. (2008). *The syntax of (anti-)causatives: External arguments in change-of-state contexts.* Amsterdam: John Benjamins.

Sun, C. (1996). Transitivity, the *ba*-construction and its history. *Journal of Chinese Linguistics, 23*(1), 159–195.

Sybesma, R. (1992). *Causatives and accomplishments: The case of Chinese ba.* Doctoral dissertation. Leiden University.

Sybesma, R. (1999). *The Mandarin VP.* Dordrecht & Boston: Kluwer.

Tai, H. (2003). Cognitive relativism: Resultative construction in Chinese. *Language and Linguistics, 4*(2), 301–316.

Tenny, C. & Pustejovsky, J. (2000). A history of events in linguistic theory. In C. Tenny, & J. Pustejovsky (Eds.), *Events as grammatical objects: The converging perspectives of lexical semantics and syntax* (pp. 3–32). Stanford: CSLI Publications.

Travis, L. (2010). *Inner aspect: The articulation of VP.* Dordrecht: Springer.

van Hout, A. (1996). *Event semantics of verb frame alternations.* Doctoral dissertation. Tilburg University.

Vendler, Z. (1967). *Linguistics in philosophy.* Ithaca: Cornell University Press.

von Stechow, A. (1996). The different readings of *wieder* 'again': A structural account. *Journal of Semantics, 13,* 87–138.

Wang, C. (2010). *The microparametric syntax of resultatives in Chinese languages.* Doctoral dissertation. New York University.

Wood, J. (2012). *Icelandic morphosyntax and argument structure.* Doctoral dissertation. New York University.

Zhang, N. (2001). The structures of depictive and resultative constructions in Chinese. *ZAS Papers in Linguistics, 22,* 191–221.

Ziegeler, D. (2000). A possession-based analysis of the *ba*-construction in Mandarin Chinese. *Lingua, 110,* 807–842.

Zou, K. (1993). The syntax of the Chinese *ba* construction. *Journal of Linguistics, 31,* 715–736.

Zou, K. (1994). Resultative V-V compounds in Chinese. In H. Harley, & P. Colin (Eds.), *MIT Working Papers in Linguistics* 22 (Vol. 22, pp. 271–290).

Chapter 4
The External Argument and Alternations of V-V Resultatives

4.1 Introduction

In Chap. 3, I argued that the two subclasses of V-V resultatives, object-oriented and subject-oriented resultatives, have different syntactic structures, though they have the same V-V surface form, and both convey the resultative meaning. I argued that object-oriented V-V resultatives are transitive causatives, while subject-oriented V-V resultatives are unaccusative inchoative predicates, and that the primary difference between them is the presence/absence of the v_{CAUSE} head. The basic syntactic structures of the two types of V-V resultatives are illustrated in (1) and (2).

(1) a. Object-oriented V-V resultative
    John **kan-dao**-le na-ke shu.
    John cut-fall-ASP that-CL tree
    'John cut down that tree.'

b. Subject-oriented V-V resultative
    John **zou-lei**-le.
    John walk-be.tired-ASP
    'John got tired from walking.'

(2) a. Object-oriented resultatives   b. Subject-oriented resultatives

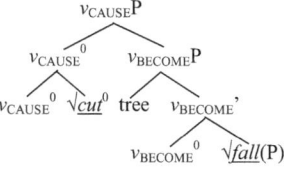

In this chapter I have two goals. The first is to examine the properties of the subject in these two constructions. I demonstrate that the subject of an object-oriented resultative is an external argument—an argument that is not introduced by the verb that semantically requires it, but is introduced by functional head, while the subject of a subject-oriented resultative is not. I thus provide further support for the analysis that the two types of V-V resultatives have different structures. In demonstrating subject properties, I relate them to two theories of the differences between causatives and non-causatives, namely, those of Pylkkänen (2008), and Alexiadou, Anagnostopoulou, and Schäfer (2015).

© The Author(s), under exclusive license to Springer Nature Singapore Pte Ltd. 2021   91
J. Liu, *The Syntax of V-V Resultatives in Mandarin Chinese*,
https://doi.org/10.1007/978-981-33-6846-0_4

Regarding the structures of causatives and non-causatives, different analyses are proposed in the literature. Pylkkänen (2008) proposes that what universally distinguishes causative verbs from their noncausative counterparts is a causing event argument, and that causative constructions involve the syntactic head Cause, which is absent in non-causatives. Other recent work (Alexiadou, Anagnostopoulou, & Schäfer, 2015; Schäfer, 2008), in contrast, posits that both causatives and noncausatives contain a causative event semantically, and both contain the v_{CAUSE} head in their syntactic structure; they differ only in the presence (in causatives) versus absence (in noncausatives) of the VoiceP. In Chap. 3, I argued for the existence of v_{CAUSE} in object-oriented resultatives, which I analyzed as causative constructions, and the absence of this head from subject-oriented resultatives, which I argued to be unaccusative constructions. My analysis is thus consistent with Pylkkänen's analysis. In this chapter, I will demonstrate that the subject in object-oriented resultatives is an external argument, while in subject-oriented resultatives it is not, thus compatible with the two above-mentioned analyses.

My second goal in this chapter is to explore the alternation properties of V-V resultatives. One property of V-V resultatives in Mandarin is that some of them can appear in alternative argument structures. Notably, when appearing in alternative argument structures, these expressions demonstrate complex properties. For example, the V-V resultative *zhui-lei* 'chase-be tired' is usually used as an object-oriented resultative, as illustrated in (3a). *Zhui-lei* 'chase-be tired', however, also has a subject-oriented, intransitive use, at least for some speakers. This use is shown in (3b).

(3) a. Normal transitive use
    John **zhui-lei**-le   Bill.
    John chase-be.tired-ASP Bill
    'John chased Bill so that Bill got tired.'

    b. Alternative intransitive use
    John **zhui-lei**-le   Bill.
    John chase-be.tired-ASP Bill
    'John chased Bill so that John got tired.'

The two uses of *zhui-lei* 'chase-be tired' correspond to two different argument structures, and the non-canonical subject/object mapping of the two DPs for V_1 is still under debate.[1]

A second complex property is illustrated in (4). The V-V resultative compound *he-zui* 'drink-be drunk', which is normally used as an intransitive (4a), can also be used as a transitive (4b). Notably, when used as a transitive, its subject is under certain restrictions (4c), the nature of which is still unclear. Despite much discussion, how to account for these properties has remained an issue up until now.

---

[1] For some authors (e.g., Han, 2017; Her, 2007; Li, 1990, 1995), this expression has a third reading, which is 'Bill chased John so that Bill got tired.' Like some other authors (Zhang, 2001, for example), I judge this interpretation as unavailable, and I leave the investigation and analysis of this reading for future research.

(4) a. Intransitive use
   John **he-zui**-le.
   John drink-be.drunk-ASP
   'John drank and got drunk.'

   b. Transitive use
   na ping jiu **he-zui**-le John.
   that bottle wine drink-be.drunk-ASP John
   'That bottle of wine got John drunk.'

   c. Transitive use
   *yumen-de xinqing **he-zui**-le John.
   depressed mood drink-be.drunk-ASP John
   Intended meaning: 'The depressed feeling made John drunk from drinking.'

Moreover, the following fundamental questions regarding the alternation of resultative V-V compounds have not been addressed to date:

(I)   Why do only a very small number of V-V resultative compounds have alternative uses,
      while the majority do not?
(II) For the alternating compounds, what allows them to alternate? What are the restrictions
      they are subject to when alternating?
(III) Why do the alternated uses of some V-V resultatives tend to be marginal?

In this chapter, I propose an analysis of all these issues, within which all the above-mentioned properties and questions can receive a unified account. My analysis crucially invokes the analysis from Chap. 3 that the two subtypes of V-V resultatives, object-oriented and subject-oriented V-V resultatives, have different syntactic structures. In previous analyses which assume that all the resultative constructions have the same syntactic structure (e.g., Huang, 2006; Li, 1990, 1993; Lin, 2004; Wang, 2010), there is no fundamental difference between the alternations of different resultative V-V compounds, and the alternations seems largely arbitrary. However, from the analysis that the two subclasses of V-V resultatives have different structures, a substantial difference appears immediately. Because the two subtypes of resultatives fall into two categories—transitive causatives (object-oriented resultatives) and unaccusatives (subject-oriented resultatives)—their alternations actually are of different natures, and fall into two categories: decausativization of causatives (object-oriented resultatives), and causativization of unaccusatives (subject-oriented resultatives). I will demonstrate that this approach, together with the Direct Causation Condition, provides a principled and unified account of the relevant alternation properties.

This chapter is organized as follows. Section 4.2 focuses on the properties of the subject in the two types of V-V resultatives. Before presenting these properties in Sect. 4.2.2, I will first review the two analyses of the structures of causatives versus noncausatives mentioned above, namely those of Pylkkänen (2008) and Alexiadou, Anagnostopoulou, and Schäfer (2015), in Sect. 4.2.1. Section 4.3 presents my analysis of the alternation properties of V-V resultatives. Section 4.4 concludes the chapter.

4.2   The Properties of the Subject of V-V Resultatives

4.2.1   Theoretical Background: The Different Structures of Causatives and Noncausatives

The causative/noncausative alternation[2] is an argument-structure-alternation found in most (if not all) languages, as illustrated in (5)–(7) below.

(5) English
  a. Noncausative   b. Causative
  The window broke.   Lisa broke the window.

(6) Japanese
  a. Noncausative
  Yasai-ga   kusa-tta.
  vegetable-NOM rot-PAST
  'The vegetable rotted.'

  b. Causative
  Taroo-ga yasai-o   kus-ase-ta.
  Taro-NOM vegetable-ACC rot-CAUSE-PAST
  'Taro caused the vegetable to rot.'

                                        (Pylkkänen, 2008, p. 120)
(7) Greek
  a. Noncausative
  I supa   kaike.
  the soup-NOM burnt-NAct-3SG
  'The soup burnt.'

  b. Causative
  O Janis   ekapse ti supa.
  the John-NOM burnt-3SG soup-ACC
  'John burnt the soup.'

                                        (Alexiadou, 2014, p. 22)

Current analysis of this alternation within an event-based model of argument structure generally hypothesizes two separate functional heads on top of the $\sqrt{P}$ in causatives: the head v_{CAUSE}, which is responsible for causative/eventive semantics, and the head Voice, which introduces the external argument (Harley, 2008, 2013; Kratzer, 1996; Marantz, 2013; Pylkkänen, 2008). On the other hand, recent studies differ with regard to how causatives and noncausatives differ semantically and syntactically. As just mentioned, Pylkkänen (2008) argues that what universally

---

[2]In this chapter, following the literature (e.g., Pylkkänen, 2008), I use the terms *causative* and *noncausative* to refer to the pairs such as in (5)–(7). The transitive verb is called a (*direct*) *causative*, and the term *noncausative* is meant to refer to the intransitive use of the verb in which the subject corresponds to the object of the causative counterpart. By the terms *causative* and *noncausative*, I simply refer to the transitive and intransitive variants of the alternation, and do not reflect any theoretical assumptions about the derivational or morphological relationship between them.

distinguishes causative verbs from their noncausative counterparts is a causing event argument; all causative constructions involve the head Cause, which noncausative predicates lack. Other recent work (Alexiadou, Anagnostopoulou, & Schäfer, 2015), in contrast, posits that causatives and noncausative change-of-state predicates both contain a causative event and a Cause head; these two constructions differ only in the presence versus absence of the VoiceP in their syntactic structures. In what follows, I briefly review Pylkkänen (2008) and Alexiadou, Anagnostopoulou, and Schäfer (2015), as representatives of these two proposals.

4.2.1.1   Pylkkänen (2008): Causatives and Noncausatives Differ in Appearance/Absence of v_{CAUSE}

Pylkkänen (2008) focuses on the semantic and syntactic realization of the element CAUSE in direct causatives. Pylkkänen argues that causative constructions essentially "involve the head Cause, which combines with the noncausative predicate and introduces a causing event to their semantics" (p. 84). Contrary to analyses that treat causative verbs as involving a single functional head which adds both the causative semantics and a causer argument (e.g., Doron, 1999), Pylkkänen argues that these two functions are realized by two separate functional heads: a v_{CAUSE} head, which is responsible for introducing the causative meaning, and a Voice head, which introduces the causer argument.[3] Pylkkänen proposes that all causative constructions involve a v_{CAUSE} head, and that is what universally distinguishes causative verbs from their noncausative counterparts.

Pylkkänen further proposes that, while v_{CAUSE} is a functional element distinct from Voice, its realization has two parametric variations in different languages: the v_{CAUSE} can be 'bundled' together with the Voice head into a complex head, as in (8a), or it can occur as its own separate syntactic head, as shown in (8b). In the former case, which Pylkkänen terms as *Voice-bundling*, v_{CAUSE} and Voice are grouped together into a single lexical item, and consequently into one syntactic head; in the latter case, v_{CAUSE} and Voice are realized by separate functional heads, each of them heading its own projection.

(8)   a. Voice-bundling   b. Non-Voice-bundling

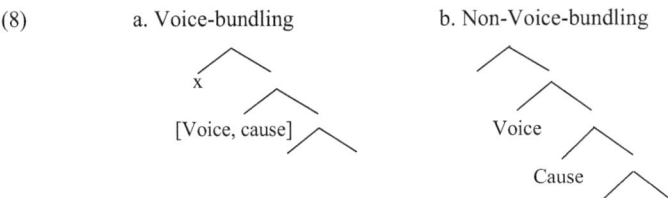

One argument of Pylkkänen's analysis, which is of particular interest to my analysis in this section, is that causatives, but not noncausatives, project both v_{CAUSE} and

---

[3] Harley (2013) gives more argumentation supporting this. Based on data from the Uto-Aztecan language Hiaki, Harley argues that the external-argument introducing projection VoiceP must be distinct from the verbalizing head little *v*, which verbalizes the root and introduces causative.

Voice (except in unaccusative causatives arguably existing in certain languages such as Japanese and Finnish, which, according to Pylkkänen, project a v_{CAUSE} head, but not a Voice head). That is to say, in most cases (i.e. except unaccusative causatives), Voice and v_{CAUSE} co-occur in causatives.

4.2.1.2 Alexiadou, Anagnostopoulou, and Schäfer (2015): Causatives and Noncausatives Differ in the Appearance/Absence of Voice

In contrast to Pylkkänen (2008), Alexiadou, Anagnostopoulou & Schäfer (hereafter AA&S) (2015) argue that causatives and noncausatives have the same event structure, both consisting of a causative event and a resultant state; the only difference between them is that an external argument and the Voice head are present in the former, but absent in the latter.

First, following previous studies, AA&S (2015) argue that causatives as well as noncausatives have one event, plus a resultant state, in their event structure. It has been proposed (e.g., Pylkkänen, 2008; von Stechow, 1996) that the event structure of both causatives and noncausatives contains one event plus a resultant state: noncausatives involve a BECOME event, as illustrated in (9), and causatives involve a CAUSE event, as in (10).[4]

(9) a. The door opened.
   b. [v-BECOME [the door √OPEN]

(10) a. John opened the door.
    b. [v-CAUSE [the door √OPEN]]

However, unlike these previous studies, AA&S (2015) crucially propose that, instead of containing a BECOME event, noncausatives actually contain a CAUSE event—just like the event in causatives. AA&S argue that, while indeed noncausative predicates lack agentivity, they do involve an inherent CAUSE meaning component in their semantics. The key argument for this proposal is that noncausatives (specifically, change-of-state predicates) can introduce (non-agentive) causer PPs. In particular, AA&S note that so-called *internally caused predicates* such as *wilt*, which are typically assumed to lack a causative variant, nonetheless introduce a causer PP, as illustrated in (11). AA&S argue that, in this respect, noncausatives like *wilt* is the

---

[4]Note that this analysis contrasts with the traditional view of the event structure of causatives and noncausatives. The traditional view, Dowty (1979) for example, maintains that for change-of-state predicates, the event structure involves a resultant state, and a BECOME predicate which takes this resultant state as its argument, as in (ia); causatives, on the other hand, have in addition a CAUSE predicate that takes the BECOME predicate as an argument and also introduces a causer argument (ib).

(i) a. [BECOME [y<STATE>]]
   b. [x CAUSE[BECOME [y<STATE>]]]

According to this view, while the event structure of change-of-state predicates involves one event, causatives involve two events.

same as externally caused change-of-state verbs like *break*, which can also introduce a non-agentive PP causer with the preposition *from*, as in (12).

(11) The flowers wilted from the heat.

(12) The window broke from the pressure.

AA&S argue that the introduction of causer PPs suggests the presence of a causative meaning component in the noncausative verbs.

While AA&S argue that noncausatives can semantically license a causer, this causer is not an external argument introduced by Voice. Instead, they maintain that the Voice head is not projected in noncausatives. AA&S claim that agents are obligatory event participants, while (non-agentive) causer PPs, in contrast, are optional event modifiers; for them, an agent is introduced by the Voice head, while a causer is dissociated from Voice. AA&S note that noncausatives lack agentivity; for example, they do not allow modification by agentive adverbials, as illustrated in (13).

(13) *The boat sank deliberately.

They also note that, unlike passives, noncausatives do not license an agent, causer, or causing event introduced by the prepositions *by* or *with*.

(14) a. The window broke (*by John)/(*with a stone).
   b. The window shattered (*by Will's banging).

AA&S therefore argue that noncausative predicates lack an implicit external argument. They take this to indicate that the Voice head is absent in noncausatives. AA&S' proposal is illustrated in (15) and (16).

(15) a. The door opened.
   b. [v-CAUSE [the door √OPEN]

(16) a. John opened the door.
   b. [John Voice [v-CAUSE [the door √OPEN]]

Comparing the proposals of Pylkkänen (2008) and AA&S (2015), the key difference between them is whether the head v_{CAUSE} is projected in noncausative constructions. In Chap. 3, I argued that the v_{CAUSE} head is absent from subject-oriented V-V resultatives, which I argued to be unaccusative predicates (noncausatives). These resultatives therefore provide support for Pylkkänen's analysis, and against that of AA&S.

On the other hand, Pylkkänen (2008) and AA&S (2015) both propose that Voice is projected in causatives.[5] In particular, AA&S (2015) propose that Voice is absent from noncausatives. In this chapter, I will demonstrate that, compatible with these analyses, in object-oriented V-V resultatives, which I analyzed as causatives, the subject is an external argument, indicating the presence of the VoiceP. In subject-oriented V-V resultatives, which I argued to be unaccusatives (noncausatives), the subject is not an external argument, indicating the absence of VoiceP.

---

[5] Except for unaccusative causatives for Pylkkänen.

4.2.2   The Properties of the Subject of Resultatives

In this section, I examine the properties of the subject in object-oriented and subject-oriented resultatives, as well as in their alternative uses. I argue that in object-oriented resultatives, the subject is an external argument, while in subject-oriented resultatives, it is a derived argument.

4.2.2.1   The External Argument in Object-Oriented V-V Resultatives

First, I argue that the DP subject in an object-oriented V-V resultative is an external argument introduced by Voice. I provide evidence from passives and from agent-oriented adverbial modification.

One diagnostic for the existence of Voice and an external argument is that a sentence containing Voice and an external argument has a passive counterpart. It has long been observed that, in many languages, sentences with a derived subject cannot be passivized (Perlmutter, 1978; Perlmutter & Postal, 1984). Current understanding assumes that passives are constructed by adding a Passive head outside VoiceP (Alexiadou, 2014; Alexiadou & Doron, 2012; Bruening, 2012; Merchant, 2013). Bruening (2012), for example, proposes that a passive clause has the basic structure in (17), in which a Pass(ive) head takes a VoiceP as complement. The VoiceP selected by Pass does not introduce an external argument DP.

(17)

One basic property of object-oriented V-V resultatives in Mandarin is that they have a passive counterpart. I illustrate this point with the examples in (18). (18a) is a V-V resultative based on *ti-kai* 'kick-open', and (18b) is the passive form of (18a), with the canonical passive morpheme in Mandarin *BEI*. In (18b), the logical object *men* 'door' is the subject, and the logical subject follows the morhoeme *BEI*, and is optional. A causer external argument is implicitly present in passive constructions, contrasting with unaccusatives, which do not imply the causer (Alexiadou, 2014; Alexiadou & Doron, 2012; Pylkkänen, 2008). Thus (18b) implies an agent, even when the optional *John* is absent. Evidence for this is that agentive adverbs are allowed, as demonstrated in (18c).

(18) a. John **ti-kai**-le   men.
         John kick-open-ASP door
         'John kicked the door open.'

      b. men bei (John) **ti-kai**-le.
         door BEI (John) kick-open-ASP
         'The door was kicked open (by John).'

      c. men bei (John) yi-jiao   **ti-kai**-le.
         door BEI (John) one.kick kick-open-ASP
         'The door was kicked open (by John) with just one kick.'

The existence of a passive counterpart thus provides evidence that the subject in an object-oriented V-V resultative is an external argument.

Another piece of evidence for the external argument analysis is that agent-oriented adverbs can occur in this construction to modify the v_{CAUSE}. As illustrated in (19) and (20), the agent-oriented adverbs, such as *jimang* 'in a hurry', *xinbuzaiyande* 'absent-mindely', *henhende* 'angrily and violently', *haobuzaihude* 'recklessly', *guyide* 'deliberately', and *shuliande* 'skillfully', *toutoumomode* 'furtively', can normally occur in object-oriented V-V resultatives. Note that, in object-oriented resultatives that contain an agent-oriented adverb, the subject can only be a human agent (19), but not an inanimate causer, as shown in (20).

(19) a. John jimang   /xinbuzaiyande /haobuzaihude **tui-kai**   men.
         John in.a.hurry/absentmindedly/recklessly   push-open door
         'John pushed the door open in a hurry/absentmindedly/recklessly.'

      b. John henhende   /guyide   **shuai-sui**-le   beizi.
         John angrily.and.violently/deliberately smash-be.broken-ASP glass
         'John smashed the glass into pieces angrily and violently/deliberately.'

(20) xiaotou shuliande /toutoumomode **qiao-kai**-le   baoxiangui.
      thief   skillfully /furtively   pry-open-ASP safe
      'The thief pried the safe open skillfully/furtively.'

(21) *feng jimang   /shuliande/guyide   **chui-kai** men.
      wind in.a.hurry/skillfully/deliberately blow-open door
      Intended meaning: 'The wind (just like a human being) blew the door open in a
                       hurry/skillfully/deliberately.'

(22) *dizhen   henhende   /haobuzaihude **zhen-sui**-le   chuangboli.
      earthquake angrily.and.violently/recklessly   shake-be.broken-ASP window.glass
      Intended meaning: 'The earthquake shattered the window glass violently/recklessly.'

Given the above properties, I argue that the subject in object-oriented V-V resultatives is an external argument. I thus conclude that object-oriented V-V resultatives in Mandarin have the structure in (23).

(23)

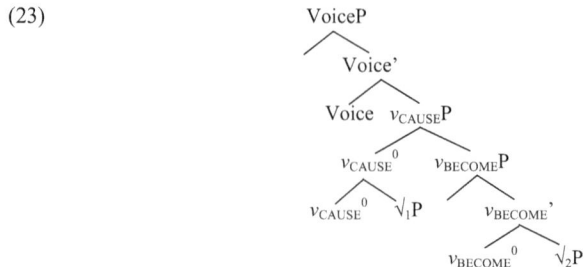

In the next section, I will demonstrate that, in subject-oriented resultatives, the subject is not an external argument. That is, the VoiceP is absent in this construction.

4.2.2.2 Subject-Oriented Resultatives: The Absence of an External Argument

In Chap. 3, I have argued that subject-oriented resultatives are syntactically unaccusative predicates. In this subsection, I provide further support for this analysis by showing that the surface subject in a subject-oriented V-V resultative is not an external argument.

First, as a basic property, subject-oriented resultatives are predominantly used as intransitive predicates, and have no passive counterparts. Given the assumption just presented that passive targets VoiceP, this is the first argument that there is no Voice or external argument in these constructions.

Further evidence for the absence of an external argument and a Voice head comes from the properties of subject-oriented resultatives with a surface object. As noted in Chap. 3, subject-oriented resultatives in Mandarin can sometimes contain a surface object, as in (24).

(24) John **chi-bao**-le   fan.
      John eat-full-ASP meal
      'John had his meal (and became) full.'

As I have demonstrated in Chap. 3, this surface object does not possess the canonical properties of a theme object. In other words, this surface object does not bear structural object Case. Burzio's (1986) proposes that the accusative Case on an object is assigned only when there is an external argument in the sentence. Kratzer (1996) also connects Voice with structural case for the object.[6] Given these proposals, I

---

[6] Note that, while Burzio's Generalization is widely invoked as a diagnostic for an external argument (e.g., Pylkkänen, 2008), an approach which I follow in the present study, it should be noted that some other authors argue against this generalization. Marantz (1991), for example, notes that there are examples in various languages that violate Burzio's Generalization. Marantz argues that, in the examples in (i), the object of *strike* is assigned accusative case, even though the subject position is non-thematic, and Burzio's generalization is thus violated.

(i) a. It struck me that I should have used 'Elmer' in this sentence.
    b. There struck me as being too many examples in his paper.   (Marantz, 1991, p. 17)

conclude that subject-oriented V-V resultatives with a surface object provide further evidence for the lack of an external argument and Voice in this construction.

Finally, a third argument for the lack of an external argument in these structures is that agent-oriented adverbs are not possible, as demonstrated in (25).

(25) a. John (*kaixinde) **chi-cheng**-le.
 John happily eat-be.overly.full-ASP
 Intended meaning: 'John got overly full from eating in a good mood.'

 b. John (*qihuhude) **zou-lei**-le.
 John angrily walk-be.tired-ASP
 Intended meaning: 'John walked angrily and got tired (from the walking).'

Given the properties presented above, I argue that, in subject-oriented resultatives, the subject is not an external argument. We can take *zou-lei* 'walk-be tired' in (26a) as an example. In this example, semantically, although John's walking event caused the result of John's being tired, syntactically the DP *John* does not function as the causer external argument of the sentence—it is rather represented as an experiencer of the event of getting tired (from walking). I thus propose that subject-oriented V-V resultatives like (26a) have the structure in (26b).

(26) a. John **zou-lei**-le.
 John walk-be.tired-ASP
 'John walked and got tired from the walking.'

 b.

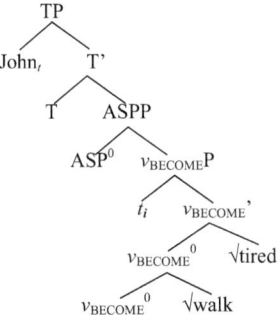

Through examining the properties of the subject in object-oriented and subject-oriented V-V resultatives, in this section I demonstrate another difference between object-oriented and subject-oriented V-V resultatives: the subject of the former is an external argument, while the subject in the latter is not. Relating this analysis to Pylkkänen (2008) and AA&S (2015), this different property between object-oriented and subject-oriented V-V resultatives in Mandarin conforms to the different property between causatives and noncausatives proposed in those two studies. In the next section, I consider another issue related to V-V resultatives in Mandarin, their alternations.

4.3   The Alternation of Resultative V-V Compounds

In this chapter, following the literature (e.g. Cheng & Huang, 1994; Huang, 2006), I use the term *alternation* to refer to the phenomenon that some V-V resultatives can occur in various argument structures. But it should be noted that for the resultatives that have an alternative use, it is not the case that there are two equally basic uses, as the term *alternation* might imply. It is indeed the case that one use is the normal and basic use, while the alternative use is just an acceptable use, or a use acceptable only to some speakers.

As briefly mentioned earlier, one property of V-V resultatives in Mandarin is that some of them can appear in a variety of argument structures. I demonstrate this phenomenon with two commonly used compounds, *xi-lou* 'wash-leak' and *he-zui* 'drink-be drunk', as examples. The object-oriented resultative *xi-lou* 'wash-leak' is normally used as a transitive predicate with two arguments: an agent subject that conducts the washing action, and a theme object—normally a container for washing, like a washbasin—which is leaky as a result of the washing action (27a). Notably, *xi-lou* 'wash-leak' can also be used as an intransitive predicate. In the intransitive use, the agent conducting the washing action is omitted, and the theme *lianpen* 'washbasin' appears in the subject position, and the predicate expresses the meaning that the theme (the washbasin) becomes leaky due to some washing action, as in (27b).

(27) a. Transitive use
     John **xi-lou**-le   lianpen.
     John wash-leak-ASP washbasin.
     'John washed clothes with the washbasin and as a result the washbasin leaked.'

    b. Intransitive use
     lianpen   **xi-lou**-le.
     washbasin wash-leak-ASP
     'The washbasin leaked as a result of being used for washing.'

Likewise, the subject-oriented resultative compound *he-zui* 'drink-be drunk' can appear in alternative argument structures. Normally *he-zui* 'drink-be drunk' is used as an intransitive (28a), conveying the meaning 'somebody gets drunk from drinking'. However, *he-zui* 'drink-be drunk' can also be used as a transitive (28b).

(28) a. Intransitive use
    John **he-zui**-le.
    John drink-be.drunk-ASP
    'John drank and got drunk.'

    b. Transitive use
    na ping jiu   **he-zui**-le   John.
    that bottle wine drink-be.drunk-ASP John
    'That bottle of wine got John drunk.'

Note that in the transitive use of *he-zui* 'drink-be drunk' (28b), a DP, which is normally restricted to wine, beer, etc., functions as the subject, and the subject in the intransitive use functions as the object. The transitive conveys the meaning 'the wine causes the object to be drunk from drinking it'.[7]

When occurring in different argument structures, Mandarin V-V resultative compounds demonstrate complex properties, some of which have received much attention in the literature (cf. Cheng & Huang, 1994; C. Li, 2008; Y. Li, 1990, 1993; Han, 2017; Huang, 2006).

The first property, as mentioned in Sect. 4.1 of this chapter, is the semantic ambiguity that occurs with V-V resultatives such as *qi-lei* 'ride-be tired' and *zhui-lei* 'chase-be tired'. As is demonstrated in (29) and (30), *qi-lei* 'ride-be tired' and *zhui-lei* 'chase-be tired' are ambiguous between two readings, which I analyze as corresponding to two different argument structures.

(29) John **qi-lei**-le   ma.
       John ride-be.tired-ASP horse
       i: 'John caused the horse to be tired by riding it.'
       ii: 'John got tired from riding the horse.'

(30) John **zhui-lei**-le   Bill.
       John chase-be.tired-ASP Bill
       i: 'John chased Bill so that Bill got tired.'
       ii: 'John chased Bill so that John got tired.'

The second property is the restriction on the subject when subject-oriented resultatives such as *he-zui* 'drink-be drunk' are alternatively used as transitives. As just mentioned, the expression *he-zui* 'drink-be drunk' is normally used as an intransitive, as illustrated in (31a). Notably, when it is used as a transitive predicate, the DP that functions as the subject is under certain restrictions. The transitive use of subject-oriented resultatives like *he-zui* 'drink-be drunk' demonstrates the following properties, as shown in (31b-c). First, the transitive use is not purely causative. As shown in (31b), in the transitive use, although the DP *na-ping jiu* 'that bottle of wine' is the subject of the sentence, as Huang (2006) notes, this sentence does not mean that that bottle of wine made John drink, and got drunk as a result, but rather, it is drinking the bottle of wine that caused John to be drunk. Second, in the transitive

---

[7]Having presented this alternation property of object-oriented and subject-oriented V-V resultatives, one interesting question is whether these alternation patterns exist with simplex verbs in Mandarin. This seems to be a complex issue. We consider simplex transitive verbs and intransitive verbs respectively. For transitive verbs, some of them, such as *xi* 'wash', demonstrate this alternation properties, as illustrated in (i), while others, such as *ti* 'kick', do not have this alternation, as illustrated in (ii).

(i) a. John zhengzai xi   yifu.   b. yifu   xi-le.
       John PROG   wash clothes   clothes wash-ASP
       'John is washing clothes.'   'The clothes have been washed.'

(ii) a. John zhengzai ti   men.   b. *men ti-le.
        John PROG   kick door   door kick-ASP
        'John is kicking the door.'   Intended meaning: 'The door was kicked (by someone).'

For intransitive verbs, it seems that none of them has the alternative transitive use, as is illustrated in (iii).

(iii) a. John zui-le.   b. *na ping jiu zui-le   John
         John be.drunk-ASP   that bottle wine be.drunk-ASP John
         'John got drunk.'   Intended meaning: 'That bottle of wine caused John to be drunk.'

use, the subject can only be an argument corresponding to the theme object of V_1 *he* 'drink', such as wine, beer, and so forth; other potential causers cannot function as the subject, as in (31c).

(31) a. Intransitive use
    John **he-zui**-le.
    John drink-be.drunk-ASP
    'John drank and got drunk.'

  b. Transitive use
    na ping jiu **he-zui**-le   John.
    that bottle wine drink-be.drunk-ASP John
    'That bottle of wine got John drunk.'

  c. Transitive use
    *yumende xinqing **he-zui**-le   John.
    depressed mood drink-be.drunk-ASP John
    Intended meaning: 'The depressed feeling made John drink and finally he got drunk.'

A third property, which to my knowledge has not been discussed in the literature, is the tight restriction on such alternations—particular for the transitive use of subject-oriented resultatives. One basic property of the alternation phenomenon is that it is far from being productive, and only a very small number of subject-oriented resultatives have an alternative use. In particular, for many (if not all) subject-oriented resultative compounds, the alternative uses are often marginal. For example, the transitive use of *he-zui* 'drink-be drunk' (31b) above, which is viewed in previous studies as a normal use of this compound (Cheng & Huang, 1994; Han, 2017; Huang, 2006), is only marginally acceptable in my judgment. Similarly, it is claimed in previous studies (e.g., Huang, 2006) that the subject-oriented resultative *ku-xing* 'cry-be awake', which is normally used as an intransitive (32a), also has the alternative transitive use as in (32b). I would judge this transitive use as unacceptable.

(32) a. xiao baobao **ku-xing**-le.
    little baby   cry-be.awake-ASP
    'The little baby cried and as a result he/she got awake.'

  b. *nage emeng   **ku-xing**-le   xiao baobao.
    that nightmare cry-be.awake-ASP little baby
    Intended meaning: 'That nightmare caused the little baby to cry and as a result
                  he/she got awake.'

To demonstrate the marginality of the alternative transitive use of subject-oriented resultative compounds, we consider one more example, the compound *chi-cheng* 'eat-be overly full'. Note that, for this compound, the normal transitive uses are barely acceptable, while the *BA* forms of these transitive uses are more acceptable, though still not completely natural, as indicated in (33).[8]

---

[8]Why the *BA* forms are more acceptable for some alternative transitive uses is not clear, but as this is not the focus of my analysis, I leave this question for future study. In relevant examples in

(33) a. John **chi-cheng**-le.
    John eat-be.overly.full-ASP
    'John got overly full by eating (too much).'

  b. ??na-dun da can   **chi-cheng**-le   John.
    that-CL big dinner eat-be.overly.full-ASP John
    'That big dinner caused John to get overly full (by eating).'

  c. ?na-dun da can   ba John **chi-cheng**-le.
    that-CL big dinner BA John eat-be.overly.full-ASP
    'That big dinner caused John to be overly full (by eating).'

Finally, in addition to these properties, one issue regarding this alternation phenomenon, which is probably even more fundamental, is that there is no proper classification and categorization for the alternations.

Corresponding to these properties, I address the following questions below:

(I)   Why do only a very small number of V-V resultative compounds have alternative uses, while the majority do not?

(II)   For the alternating compounds, what allows them to alternate? What restrictions are they subject to when alternating?

(III) Why do the alternations of some resultative V-V compounds tend to be marginal?

(IV) Is it possible to establish a system to categorize and characterize the seemingly arbitrary alternations of V-V resultatives, and thus to provide a unified account for the properties alluded to above?

In this section, I propose a new approach to the alternation properties of V-V resultatives, which I call a *causative approach*. My analysis in Chap. 3 provides a crucial precondition for this approach. In Chap. 3, I argued that, while both object-oriented and subject-oriented V-V resultatives convey cause-result semantics, they have different syntactic structures: object-oriented resultatives are causative, while subject-oriented resultatives are inchoative unaccusatives. For previous studies that assume that all resultatives have the same syntactic structure (e.g., Lin, 2004; Wang, 2010), no categorical difference is predicted between the alternations of the two subtypes of resultative V-V compounds, and their alternations largely appear to be arbitrary. From the causative approach I am proposing, however, a substantial difference appears immediately. As I will argue, since V-V resultatives fall into two categories, their alternations actually are different in nature: decausativization of causatives (object-oriented resultatives), and causativization of unaccusatives (subject-oriented resultatives). Based on this analysis, I then invoke theories developed in the causative framework—particularly, the Direct Causation Condition (McCawley, 1978; Shibatani, 1976; Wolff, 2003), to account for relevant alternation properties. In what follows, I first discuss one type of alternation, the decausativization of object-oriented V-V compounds, in Sect. 4.3.1; then I discuss the other

---

this chapter, I give the *BA* form of the transitive use when my judgment indicates that it is more acceptable.

type of alternation, the causativization of subject-oriented resultative compounds, in Sect. 4.3.2.

4.3.1 The Decausativization of Object-Oriented V-V Resultative Compounds

In one type of alternation, some canonical object-oriented V-V compounds can have an intransitive use, in which the external argument is omitted, and the internal argument function as the subject. Compounds like *xi-lou* 'wash-leak', *dun-lan* 'stew-be soft', and *ku-shi* 'cry-be wet' are reported as having this alternative use in previous studies, as shown in (34)–(36). I propose that this intransitive use actually represents the phenomenon of decausativation of object-oriented V-V resultatives, which I argued in Chap. 3 to be causative constructions.

(34) a. John **xi-lou**-le   lianpen.
      John wash-leak-ASP washbasin
      'John caused the washbasin to be leaking via washing.'

   b. lianpen   **xi-lou**-le.
      washbasin wash-leak-ASP
      'The washbasin got to be leaky via washing.'

(35) a. John **dun-lan**-le   tudou.
      John stew-be.soft-ASP potato
      'John caused the potato to be soft by stewing it.'

   b. tudou **dun-lan**-le.
      potato stew-be.soft-ASP
      'The potato got soft from being stewed.'

(36) a. John **ku-shi**-le   shoujuan.
      John cry-be.wet-ASP handkerchief
      'John cried and caused his handkerchief to be wet.'

   b. haizi ku-le   bange xiaoshi, shoujuan   dou   **ku-shi**-le.
      child cry-ASP half   hour,   handkerchief even cry-be.wet-ASP
      'The child cried for half an hour; even his handkerchief got wet.'

While these decausativized uses of V-V resultatives are generally acceptable, it should be noted that many V-V compounds do not have decausativized uses, as is illustrated in the following examples.

(37) a. qiufeng   **chui-huang**-le   shuye.
      autumn.wind blow-be.yellow-ASP leaf
      'The autumn wind blew the leaves and turned them yellow.'

    b. shuye *(bei) **chui-huang**-le.
       leaf   BEI blow-be.yellow-ASP
       Intended meaning: 'The leaves became yellow from the wind blowing.'

(38) a. John **ti-kai**-le   men.
      John kick-open-ASP door
      'John kicked the door open.'

    b. men *(bei) **ti-kai**-le.
       door BEI kick-open-ASP
       Intended meaning: 'The door opened from being kicked.'

(39) a. John **niu-duan**-le   na-tiao tie   lian.
      John twist-break-ASP that-CL iron chain
      'John broke that piece of iron chain by twisting it.'

    b. na-tiao tie   lian *(bei) **niu-duan**-le.
       that-CL iron chain BEI twist-break-ASP
       Intended meaning: 'That piece of iron chain broke from being twisted.'

What is the nature of the de-causativization in (34)–(36)? In what follows, I argue that the decausativized object-oriented V-V resultatives are unaccusative predicates that demonstrate properties similar to those of the subject-oriented V-V resultatives, both semantically and syntactically. Semantically, in the decausativized forms, the CAUSE meaning is still implied. This CAUSE meaning comes from specifying the manner of a causing event through (the root of) V_1. In terms of syntactic structure, in the decausativized forms, the v_{CAUSE} head is absent, and the root of V_1, which adjoins to the v_{CAUSE} head in the causative counterpart, here adjoins to the v_{BECOME} head. To demonstrate this, I propose that the normal transitive use and the decausativized use of *xi-lou* 'wash-leak' in (40a-b) have the syntactic structures in (41a-b), respectively.

(40) a. Normal transitive use   b. Decausativized use
     John **xi-lou**-le   lianpen.   lianpen   **xi-lou**-le.
     John wash-leak-ASP washbasin   washbasin wash-leak-ASP
     'John's washing caused the washbasin   'The washbasin got to be leaking from washing.'
     to be leaking.'

(41) a. Normal causative use   b. Decausativized use

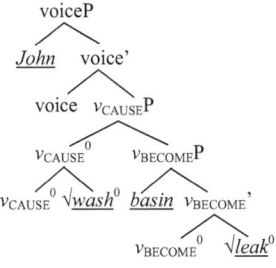
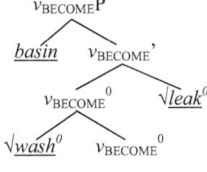

Key evidence for the decausativization analysis is the adverbial modification properties of the alternative intransitive use of object-oriented resultatives. Noticeably, in the decausativized use, the adverbs that modify v_{CAUSE} cannot occur, as demonstrated in the following examples.

(42) a. Wusong <u>san-quan liang-jiao</u>   jiu   **da-si**-le   laohu.
       Wusong three.fist two.kick   only beat-die-ASP tiger
       'Wusong beat the tiger to death by just a couple of strikes.'

     b. laohu **da-si**-le.
       tiger   beat-die-ASP
       'The tiger was killed.'

     c. *laohu san-quan liang-jiao **da-si**-le.
       tiger three.fist two.kick beat-die-ASP
       Intended meaning: 'The tiger was beat to death just by a couple of strikes.'

(43) a. John henhende   **shuai-sui**-le   beizi.
       John angrily.and.violently smash-break-ASP cup
       'John smashed the cup angrily and violently.'

     b. beiz **shuai-sui**-le.
       cup smash-break-ASP
       'The cup smashed and broke.'

     c. beizi *(bei) henhende   **shuai-sui**-le.
       cup   BEI angrily.and.violently smash-break-ASP
       Intended meaning: 'The cup was smashed by someone angrily and violently.'

These above examples indicate that the v_{CAUSE} head, which is usually projected in the object-oriented V-V resultative constructions, is absent in the alternative intransitive uses, thus providing evidence for the decausativization analysis.

4.3.2   The Causativization of Subject-Oriented Resultative V-V Compounds

As has been presented, while subject-oriented resultative V-V compounds are predominately intransitive predicates, a few of them have an alternative transitive use. In addition to the example with *he-zui* 'drink-be drunk' given in (31), repeated as (44), I provide one more example with *chi-cheng* 'eat-be overly full'. In addition to its normal intransitive use (45a), this compound can also be marginally used as a transitive, as in (45b). In the transitive use (45b), a thematic object of V_1, which does not occur with the unaccusative use, functions as the subject, and the subject of the intransitive use functions as the object of the transitive clause. Notably, as the translation of (45b) indicates, the transitive use conveys a causative meaning.

(44) a. John **he-zui**-le.
   John drink-be.drunk-ASP
   'John drank and got drunk.'

   b. na ping jiu **he-zui**-le   John.
      that bottle wine drink-be.drunk-ASP John
      'That bottle of wine got John drunk.'

(45) a. John **chi-cheng**-le   (*da-can).
   John eat-be.overly.full-ASP big dinner
   'John got overly full by eating (too much).'

   b. ? na-dun da can   ba John **chi-cheng**-le.
      that-CL big dinner BA John eat-be.overly.full-ASP
      'That big dinner caused John to get overly full (by eating).'

In Chap. 3, I argued that subject-oriented resultatives are unaccusative predicates, containing v_{BECOME} but not v_{CAUSE}. This analysis provides the basis for my analysis in this subsection. That is, if subject-oriented resultatives are unaccusative predicates, it is plausible to assume that they can be causativized. Thus I propose that there is another major category of alternations of V-V resultatives, which is the transitive use of the subject-oriented V-V resultatives, as demonstrated in (44) and (45) above. I argue that this alternation involves the causativization of this type of V-V resultative compound. In the remainder of this section, I first summarize my proposal in Sect. 4.3.2.1, and then after briefly reviewing Rappaport Hovav & Levin's (2012) work on the Direct Causation Condition in Sect. 4.3.2.2, which the present study adopts, I present my analysis in Sect. 4.3.2.3, demonstrating how this proposal can capture the properties of this class of alternations.

4.3.2.1 Summary of the proposal

I argue that the complex properties that the transitive alternations of subject-oriented resultatives demonstrate are largely due to two sources: the Direct Causation Condition on causatives, and the unique semantic and syntactic properties of this type of V-V resultatives as unaccusative predicates. While subject-oriented resultatives are syntactically unaccusatives, they differ from normal simplex unaccusative predicates in that they also specify a CAUSE in their meaning—a causing event denoted by (the root of) V_1—while a normal simplex unaccusative predicate generally does not specify this. That is, as change-of-state predicates, subject-oriented resultatives nonetheless convey a 'cause-result' meaning, and in this respect, they are semantically more like causatives. Based on this unique property, and given the Direct Causation Condition, I argue that, while syntactically it is possible for subject-oriented V-V resultative compounds to be causativized, semantically and pragmatically, their unique 'cause-result' meaning makes this causativization difficult or even impossible. As we will see in the next section, the Direct Causation Condition requires that the subject of a causative must be the direct causer, but for subject-oriented resultatives, the direct cause is already implied by V_1, and it is therefore difficult to find an appropriate DP direct causer. That is to say, in the usual case, subject-oriented V-V resultatives cannot be causativized. I argue that this explains the fact that transitive alternation of subject-oriented V-V resultatives is highly restricted, and only very few members have an alternative transitive use.

With regard to the subject-oriented resultatives that do have an alternative transitive use, I first report an observation, that is, those that have an alternative transitive use tend to have a transitive V_1, and in the transitive use, a thematic object of the transitive V_1 functions as the subject. I propose that these transitive alternations are allowed because the thematic object of V_1, as a participant of the causing event, makes a best candidate—and therefore a possible causer—to meet the Direct Causation Condition. On the other hand, it should be noted that, while the DP in question can function as an acceptable causer, they are nonetheless not the canonical causer, since in subject-oriented resultatives, the direct cause is always the causing event denoted by V_1, rather than the thematic object of V_1. I propose that this accounts for the marginality of the transitive uses of subject-oriented resultatives.

In what follows, I demonstrate how this approach can capture the properties of V-V resultative alternations. As my analysis crucially invokes the Direct Causation Condition, I first present this condition by reviewing Rappaport Hovav & Levin (2012).

4.3.2.2   Direct Causation Condition: Rappaport Hovav & Levin (2012)

It has long been established that lexical causatives indicate direct causation, contrasting with periphrastic causatives, which can describe instances of either direct or indirect causation (Fodor, 1970; McCawley, 1978; Shibatani, 1976; Wolff, 2003).[9] Based on this fundamental property of lexical causatives, it is generally agreed that in introducing the external argument in lexical causatives, one major constraint is the so-termed *Direct Causation Condition*, which requires that the lexical causatives should indicate direct causation (Bittner, 1999; Fodor, 1970; McCawley, 1978; Shibatani, 1976; Vecchiato, 2011; Wolff, 2003). In what follows, I present this condition by reviewing the analysis of Rappaport Hovav & Levin (hereafter R&L) (2012).

Studies of the causative alternation, illustrated in (46), have largely been concerned with two questions: first, is one variant of the alternation basic? Secondly, is there a lexical rule that derives the other variant from the basic variant?

(46) a. The door opened. [Anticausative variant]
    b. John opened the door. [Causative variant]

As a background to R&L's (2012) analysis, one class of previous studies has proposed a decausativization analysis of the alternation (e.g., Levin & Rappaport Hovav, 1995; Reinhart, 2002). These authors argue that alternating verbs are lexically associated with two arguments, a causer subject and a theme object; of the two variants, the causative variant is basic, and the noncausative variant is derived from the

---

[9]For a different view, see Neeleman & van de Koot (2002).

causative variant via a lexical arity operation of decausativization, which eliminates the causer argument.

Contrary to this earlier analysis, R&L (2012) propose that the noncausative variant is basic, and the causative variant is formed by adding a causer argument to the noncausative predicate. R&L further argue that the causer arguments are not lexically specified by the alternating verbs, rather, their properties—specifically, when a causer can appear and what qualifies as an acceptable causer, are determined by an extra-lexical factor—the Direct Causation Condition. R&L's proposal is mainly based on their observation of the causative alternation properties of two groups of verbs, internally caused change-of-state verbs and calibratable change-of-state verbs.

Internally caused change-of-state verbs, such as *blossom*, *rust*, and *wilt*, generally denote a change of state for which the means of bringing about the change are inherent and internal properties of the entity undergoing the change. While internally caused change-of-state verbs are predominantly used as intransitives, R&L claim that they also have causative uses, as illustrated in (47).

(47) a. Early summer heat blossomed fruit trees across the valley.
　　 b. Salt air rusted the chain-link fences.　　　　　　　　　　(L&R, 2012, p. 161)

R&L note that one property of the causative alternation of internally caused change-of-state verbs is that the subject of the causative variant is restricted: it is normally a natural force, as is shown in (47) above, but cannot be an agent, as is shown in (48) below.

(48) a. *The farmer/the new fertilizer blossomed the fruit trees.
　　 b. *The careless gardener rusted the fence with a misplaced sprinkler.
　　　　　　　　　　　　　　　　　　　　　　　　　　　(L&R, 2012, p. 161)

Like internally caused change-of-state verbs, verbs like *skyrocket*, *plummet*, *plunge*, which R&L call *verbs of calibratable change-of-state*, are most often used as intransitives. However, R&L claim that verbs of this group also have causative uses under certain restricted conditions, as illustrated in (49).

(49) a. Solving this issue skyrocketed my personal growth.
　　 b. I wouldn't say being on Tara has skyrocketed my career.
　　 c. I woke up this morning to rain and strong winds that have plummeted the temperature.
　　　　　　　　　　　　　　　　　　　　　　　　　　(L&R, 2012, p. 163)

R&L note that one property of the causative alternation for these verbs is that they only have a causative variant for certain subject-object combinations—that is, the choice of subject depends on the choice of object, a phenomenon that R&L term *subject-object interdependency*. R&L report two cases of such subject-object interdependency. In the first case, as shown in (49) above, when the theme objects of these examples are properties inalienably possessed by an animate entity, such as *growth*, *career*, or *confidence*, the subjects are events or states. In the second case, when the subjects are agents and the objects are properties inalienably possessed by an animate entity, some such combinations are allowed, as shown in (50a), while others are not, as in (50b). The attested causative uses of verbs of calibratable change of state as in (49) and (50), according to R&L, indicate that the semantic type of subject argument depends on the kind of theme occurring with it.

(50) a. Henderson skyrocketed his career by sinking a choke in the third.
  b. *My mother skyrocketed my personal growth.

(L&R, 2012, p. 168)

Based on these data, R&L argue for the following two points. First, if the causative variant is basic and anticausative uses are derived from the causative uses, it is difficult to explain the phenomenon that internally caused change of state verbs and calibratable change of state verbs are predominantly used as anticausatives and have only restricted causative uses. R&L therefore propose that the anticausative use is the basic form, and the causative use involves adding a causer argument to the anticausative predicate.

R&L's second argument, which is of particular relevance to my study, is that the nature of the causers is determined non-lexically. Following previous work (e.g., Fodor, 1970; McCawley, 1978; Shibatani, 1976; Wolff, 2003), R&L propose that the causer is subject to the Direct Causation Condition, which they define as follows:

> The Direct Causation Condition: A single-argument verb may be expressed in a clause as a transitive verb if the subject represents a direct cause of the event expressed by the verb and its argument. (R&L, 2012, p. 160).

For direct causation, R&L adopt the definition of Wolff's (2003) *no-intervening-cause hypothesis*, which proposes that direct causation is present between the causer and the final causee in a causal chain if there are no intermediate causers between them. R&L claim that the availability of a causative use of a verb depends on whether the cause meets this condition.

R&L (2012) demonstrates that the causative alternation properties of internally caused change-of-state verbs and verbs of calibratable change-of-state described above all follow from the Direct Causation Condition. First, for the internally caused change-of-state verbs, as just introduced, the subjects of their causative uses are normally natural force, but not agents. R&L argue that this is because, given the nature of this group of verbs, natural force or ambient condition are the most immediate causes of such eventualities; an agent, which does not have control over this change, would have to precede a natural force or ambient condition in the chain of causation. R&L argue that this explains the acceptability of the sentences in (47), repeated as (51), and the unacceptability of (48), repeated as (52).

(51) a. Early summer heat blossomed fruit trees across the valley.
  b. Salt air rusted the chain-link fences.

(R&L, 2012, p. 161)

(52) a. *The farmer/the new fertilizer blossomed the fruit trees.
  b. *The careless gardener rusted the fence with a misplaced sprinkler.

(L&R, 2012, p. 167)

R&L argue that the subject-object interdependencies shown by the causative use of verbs of calibratable change-of-state can also receive an account based on the Direct Causation Condition. For example, they propose that changes in the values of properties inherently possessed by animate entities are like internally caused changes of state: they are generally only under the control of the possessor, and a third party cannot directly manipulate them. This accounts for the acceptability of (53a), where the agent subject *Henderson* is the possessor of the object *career*, and the unacceptability of (53b), where the agent my *mother* is not the possessor of the theme *my personal growth*.

(53) a. Henderson skyrocketed his career by sinking a choke in the third.
   b. *My mother skyrocketed my personal growth.

My analysis of the alternation of V-V resultative compounds in Mandarin adopts this Direct Causation Condition, as formulated in R&L (2012). In the next section, I will demonstrate that like the two groups of verbs in English, Mandarin subject-oriented resultatives, which are predominantly used as unaccusative, also have restricted causative uses, and crucially, their causativization is also subject to the Direct Causation Condition.

4.3.2.3 The Alternation Properties of Subject-Oriented V-V Resultatives: My Analysis

As just mentioned, a most conspicuous property of the alternative transitive/causative use of subject-oriented resultatives is that this type of alternations is highly restricted—only a very small number of examples are attested—and the majority of subject-oriented resultatives do not allow a transitive/causative use. For example, subject-oriented resultatives like *pao-diu* 'run-be lost', *zhan-ma* 'stand-be numb', *zou-lei* 'walk-be tired', and *ku-yun* 'cry-be dizzy' do not allow a causative use.

In Chap. 3, I argued that subject-oriented V-V resultatives are unaccusative predicates, which have the syntactic structure in (54). In this structure, the root of V_1 adjoins to the v_{BECOME} head as a modifier, and the functional head v_{BECOME} takes the root of V_2 as its complement. Semantically, this structure is interpreted as 'the subject comes into the state described by the root of V_2 ($\sqrt{2}$) in the manner described by the root of V_1 ($\sqrt{1}$).

(54)

$$v_{BECOME}P$$
$$v_{BECOME}^0 \quad \sqrt{2}^0$$
$$\sqrt{1}^0 \quad v_{BECOME}^0$$

It should be noted that, as unaccusative predicates, one difference of subject-oriented V-V resultatives from simplex unaccusative predicates is that they also specify the cause of the becoming event—via the root of V_1. We demonstrate this difference by comparing the simplex unaccusative predicate *lei* 'be tired' (55a) and the subject-oriented V-V resultatiave *zou-lei* 'walk-be tired' (55b). Note that the simplex predicate in (55a) only specifies the state (*be tired*) that the subject comes into, and does not indicate the cause for the 'be-tired' state. I assume that (55a) has the syntactic structure in (56a). In contrast, in the subject-oriented resultative (55b), in addition to indicating the state that the subject comes into via the root of V_2 (*lei* 'be tired'), this predicate also specifies the cause for the 'be-tired' event, via the root of V_1. I have proposed that syntactically this is realized by having the root of V_1 modify the v_{BECOME} head as a manner of the 'becoming' event, as shown in (56b). Semantically, the meaning of the sentence is that 'John got tired from walking', as indicated by the translation of (55b). That is, the walking event is the cause of the 'be-tired' event.

(55) a. Simplex unaccusative   b. Unaccusative of subject-oriented V-V resultative
     John **lei**-le.   John **zou-lei**-le.
     John be.tired-ASP   John walk-be.tired-ASP
     'John was/got tired.'   'John got tired from walking.'

(56) a.   b.

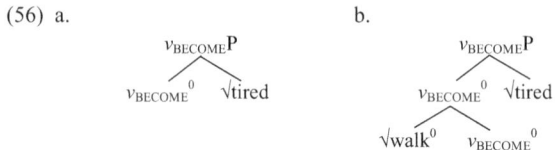

On the other hand, following Pylkkänen (2008), I assume that, in terms of syntax, to causativize the unaccusative predicate syntactically is to add a v_{CAUSE}P on top of the v_{BECOME}P, as well as a VoiceP introducing a direct causer at its specifier, as schematized in (57). I therefore propose that (57) is the syntactic structure of the alternative transitive uses of subject-oriented resultative compounds.

(57)

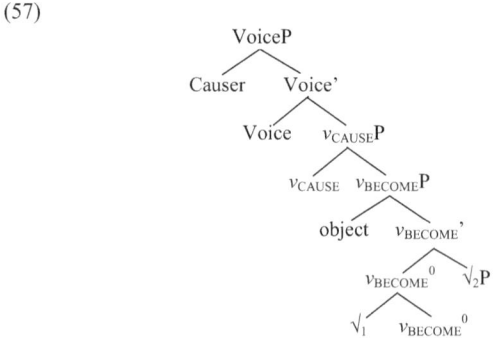

One point to note, which is important for my analysis, is that the structure in (57) only expresses the meaning 'cause to become the state of V_2 in the manner of V_1', but crucially not the meaning 'cause to do the V_1 event and then become the state of V_2'. We consider the example *zou-lei* 'walk-be tired' again. If *zou-lei* can be causativized, the causative structure can only mean that a direct causer causes John to become tired in the manner of walking; it cannot mean that a direct causer causes John to walk and then become tired.

Causativization of subject-oriented resultatives thus possesses an important difference from the causative object-oriented resultatives—while the former is the causativization of V-V resltative, the latter is causativization of a simplex unaccusative predicate (normally containing a single V). I demonstrate this difference by comparing *he-zui* 'drink-be drunk' and *kan-dao* 'cut-fall'. Note that, while the alternative transitive use of the subject-oriented resultative compound *he-zui* 'drink-be drunk' can be viewed as the causativization of the whole compound, the object-oriented V-V resultative *kan-dao* 'cut-fall' is the causativization of just the unaccusative predicate *dao* 'fall'. Syntactically, in object-oriented resultatives, the root of V_1 adjoins to v_{CAUSE}, while in causativization of subject-oriented resultatives, the root of V_1 adjoins to v_{BECOME}. This difference between them is illustrated in (58) and (59) below.

(58) a. Causative object-oriented resultative   b. Causativization of subject-oriented resultative

    John **kan-dao**-le shu.   na-ping   jiu   **he-zui**-le   John.
    John cut-fall-ASP tree   that-bottle wine drink-be.drunk-ASP John
    'John cut down a tree.'   'That bottle of wine caused John to be drunk
                             (from drinking it).'

(59) a. Object-oriented resultative   b. Causativization of subject-oriented resultative

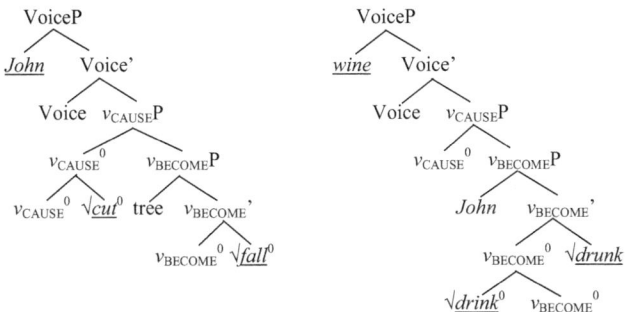

Note that in (59b), the subject *na-ping jiu* 'that bottle of wine', the selection of which is semantically subject to the DCC, is syntactically introduced by the Voice head. Also, in both (59a-b), the verbal root $\sqrt{2}$ ($\sqrt{fall}$ and $\sqrt{drunk}$), after merging with the v_{BECOME} head, raises to the position next to the verbal root $\sqrt{1}$ through head-movement, deriving the surface string.

We now consider how the relevant alternation properties of subject-oriented resultatives can be captured. First, the property that the alternative causative use of these V-V compounds is highly restricted. To account for this property, I propose that due to the Direct Causation Condition, and also due to the semantic and syntactic properties of subject-oriented resultatives, the causativization of subject-oriented V-V resultatives is actually impossible in most cases. That is to say, while the unaccusative syntactic structure makes it theoretically possible for subject-oriented V-V resultatives to be causativized, their special 'cause-result' semantics makes this causativization practically difficult or even impossible. On the one hand, due to the Direct Causation Condition, one basic requirement for a subject-oriented resultative V-V compound to be able to causativize is to find a direct cause for the resultant 'becoming event', and a DP causer that can function as the subject of the causativized construction. On the other hand, given that subject-oriented resultatives already specify direct cause, it is difficult, or impossible, to find such a DP. For example, in the case of *zou-lei* 'walk-be tired', the direct cause for the 'being tired' event is the walking event. In this situation, it is impossible to find another direct causer. As another example, we consider the scenario that a coach asked John to walk until he (John) got tired. For this situation, Mandarin speakers cannot say the sentence in (60). In my analysis, this is because, while the coach is the direct cause of John's walking, the direct cause for John's being tired is the walking event, not the coach.

(60) *jiaolian **zou-lei**-le   John.
       coach   walk-be.tired-ASP John
       Intended meaning: 'The coach caused John to walk and as a result John got tired.'

I argue that this explains why the majority of subject-oriented V-V resultatives do not have an alternative transitive/causative use.

We now consider the subject-oriented resultatives that do have an alternative transitive use. In Mandarin subject-oriented V-V resultatives, V_1 can be an intransitive verb, such as *pao* 'run' in (61a), or a transitive verb, such as *he* 'drink' in (61b).

(61) a. xiaogou **pao-diu**-le.
          puppy   run-be.missing-ASP
          'The puppy ran around, and finally it went missing.'

     b. John **he-zui**-le.
        John drink-be.drunk-ASP
        'John drank and got drunk.'

One observation of this study is that the availability of a transitive alternation of a resultative seems to be related to the transitivity of V_1 of the resultative. Specifically, when V_1 is an intransitive verb, the compound tends not to have an alternative transitive use. For example, the compounds in (62)–(64), which have intransitive V_1, do not have transitive alternations.

(62) a. xiaogou **pao-diu**-le.
  puppy   run-be.missing-ASP
  'The puppy ran around, and finally it went missing.'

  b. *kaixinde wan-er/fuzade   dixing/moshengde huanjing   **pao-diu**-le   xiaogou.
   happy   play /complex terrain/unfamiliar environment run-be.missing-ASP puppy
   Intended meaning: 'A happy time/complex terrain/unfamiliar environment caused the
                   puppy to be lost after running around.'

(63) a. John de   tui **zhan-ma**-le.
   John DE (possessive) leg stand-be.numb-ASP
   'John's legs became numb from standing.'

  b. *shouyinyuan de   gongzuo **zhan-ma**-le   John de   tui.
   cashier   DE (possessive) work   stand-be.numb-ASP John DE (possessive) leg
   Intended meaning: 'Working as a cashier caused John's legs to become numb
                   from standing.'

  c. ??changshijiande lüxing **zhan-ma**-le   John de   tui.
   long-time   travel stand-be.numb-ASP John DE (possessive) leg
   Intended meaning: 'Extended travel caused John's legs to become numb
                   from standing.'
   [John had to stand on the coach during the travel.]

(64) a. shu **zhang-wai**-le.
   tree grow-be.slanting-ASP
   'The tree gets to be slanting after (or as a result of) growing.'

  b. *yuanding/zhouweide zhedangwu **zhang-wai**-le   zhe-ke shu.
   gardener /around   shelter   grow-be.slanting-ASP this-CL tree
   Intended meaning: 'The gardener/the shelter around caused the tree to grow into a
                   slanting posture.'

These examples indicate that, when V_1 is an intransitive verb, the resultative V-V
compounds cannot be causativized.

On the other hand, V-V resultatives with a transitive V_1 may have a transi-
tive/causative alternation, as demonstrated in the following examples.

(65) a. John **he-zui**-le.
       John drink-be.drunk-ASP
       'John drank and got drunk.'

   b. na-ping jiu **he-zui**-le   John.
      that-bottle wine drink-be.drunk-ASP John
      'That bottle of wine caused John to be drunk.'

(66) a. John de   yanjing **kan-hua**-le.
       John DE (possessive) eye   read-be.blurred-ASP
       'John's eyes got blurred from reading the newspapar (intensively).'

   b. baozhi   **kan-hua**-le   John de   yanjing.
      newspaper read-be.blurred-ASP John DE (possessive) eye
      '(Reading) newspapers caused John's eyes to become blurred.'

(67) a. moshubiaoyan tai jingcai-le,   guanzhong dou **kan-dai**-le.
       magic.show   so wonderful-ASP audience   even watch-be.stunned-ASP
       'The magic show was so wonderful that the audience watching it was stunned.'

   b. nage jingcaide moshubiaoyan ba guanzhong dou   **kan-dai**-le.
      that wonderful magic show   BA audience even watch-be.stunned-ASP
      'That wonderful magic show caused the audience to be stunned.'

(68) a. kenrenmen **chi-tu**-le.
       guests   eat-vomit-ASP
       'The guests ate and as a result vomited.'
       [In the context that the guests ate unclean food, or ate too much.]

   b. na-dun haixian ba suoyoude keren dou **chi-tu**-le.
      that-CL seafood BA all   guest all eat-vomit-ASP
      'That seafood dinner caused all the guests to vomit after eating.'

Each of the above examples contains a transitive V_1, and these resultatives have a causative counterpart, as shown in the (b) examples.

The V-V resultatives that have a transitive V_1 and a causative counterpart demonstrate still another property: the alternation is subject to further constraints on the properties of the causer subject. For the causativized V-V resultatives in (66)–(68), the subject can only be a thematic object of V_1, not some other logically possible causer. To demonstrate this, let us consider *he-zui* 'drink-be drunk' and *chi-cheng* 'eat-be overly full'. For *he-zui* 'drink-be drunk' (69), the DP *na-ping jiu* 'that bottle of wine', which is the theme of V_1 *he* 'drink', makes a good causer subject, while another DP *yumende xinqing* 'depressed mood', which bears no thematic relation to V_1 *he* 'drink', cannot function as the subject of the causative use. The example in (70) demonstrates a parallel situation with *chi-cheng* 'eat-be overly full'.

(69) a. John **he-zui**-le.
    John drink-be.drunk-ASP
    'John drank and got drunk.'

    b. na-ping   jiu   **he-zui**-le   John.
    that-bottle wine drink-be.drunk-ASP John
    'That bottle of wine caused John to be drunk.'

    c. *yumende xinqing **he-zui**-le   John.
    depressed mood   drink-be.drunk-ASP John
    Intended meaning: 'The depressed feeling made John drunk from drinking.'

(70) a. John **chi-cheng**-le.
    John eat-be.overly.full-ASP
    'John got overly full by eating (too much).'

    b. na-dun da can   ba John **chi-cheng**-le.
    that-CL big dinner BA John eat-be.overly.full-ASP
    'That big dinner caused John to get overly full by eating (too much).'

    c. *John de   mama ba John **chi-cheng**-le.
    John DE (possessive) mother BA John eat-be.overly.full-ASP
    Intended meaning: 'John's mother caused John to get overly full by eating (too much).'

I argue that, one reason that the alternative transitive uses of these resultatives are acceptable is that the theme object of V_1 is acceptable as a direct causer, because they are part of the causing event. We consider the example *he-zui* 'drink-be drunk'. This example is claimed in various previous analyses (e.g. Cheng & Huang, 1994; Han, 2017; Huang, 2006) to allow the causative alternation; the present analysis assumes the same judgment. In this example, while it is the wine-drinking action that directly makes John drunk, it is also true that the wine makes John drunk— at least for some speakers. In contrast, *yumende xinqing* 'depressed mood' cannot function as the causer because, while it can be the direct causer for John's drinking action, it is not the direct causer for John's getting drunk. The example in (70) can receive a similar analysis. In this example, the thematic relation to V_1 *chi* 'eat' makes the DP *na-dun dacian* 'that big dinner' an acceptable causer for the event of 'being overly full (through eating)', and therefore this DP can function as the subject of the causativized use of *chi-cheng* 'eat-be overly full', while *John de mama* 'John's mother', who fails to be a direct causer, cannot be the subject of the causativized use.[10]

Again, note that in (69) and (70) above, while 'that bottle of wine' and 'that big dinner' can be acceptable direct causers, they are not the canonical direct cause anyway, as the direct cause is always the event denoted by the root of V_1. I assume this is the source of their marginality.

---

[10]Zhang (personal communication) notes that an alternative analysis of the examples in (69) and (70) is that the subject in these examples can be a verb phrase, 'drinking that bottle of wine' in (69) and 'eating that big dinner' in (70), rather than just the DP theme of V_1, and the initial verb is deleted. While this can be a potential direction to explore, the present work so far has not found any evidence pointing to this alternative analysis, and I leave this for future work.

4.4 Conclusion

In this chapter I focused on the properties of the subject in object-oriented and subject-oriented resultatives, and the alternation properties of these constructions. I have shown that, while the subject in object-oriented resultatives is an external argument, it is a derived subject in subject-oriented resultatives. These different properties of the subject further support my analysis in Chap. 3 that object-oriented and subject-oriented resultatives have different structures.

In my analysis of alternation properties, I first proposed a categorization system for the two types of alternations—decausativization of object-oriented resultatives, and causativization of subject-oriented resultatives—and then accounted for the alternation properties that these resultatives demonstrate. I proposed that these complex properties have two sources, the Direct Causation Condition on causatives, and the particular semantic and syntactic properties of subject-oriented resultatives as unaccusative predicates with a cause syntactically expressed as an adjoined root. I have shown that this analysis not only captures the alternation properties discussed in the literature, but also captures some properties that haven't been discussed in previous studies, such as the marginality of the altenrative transitive/causative use of most subject-oriented V-V resultatives.

References

Alexiadou, A. (2014). Active, middle, and passive: The morpho-syntax of Voice. *Catalan Journal of Linguistics, 13,* 19–40.
Alexiadou, A., Anagnostopoulou, E., & Schäfer, F. (2015). *External arguments in transitivity alternations: A layering approach.* Oxford: Oxford University Press.
Alexiadou, A., & Doron, E. (2012). The syntactic construction of two non-active Voices: Passive and middle. *Journal of Linguistics, 48,* 1–34.
Bittner, M. (1999). Concealed causatives. *Natural Language Semantics, 7,* 1–78.
Bruening, B. (2012). By-phrases in passives and nominals. *Syntax, 16,* 1–41.
Burzio, L. (1986). *Italian syntax: A government-binding approach.* Dordrecht: Reidel.
Cheng, L., & Huang, C.-T. (1994). On the argument structure of resultative compounds. In Y. Chen, J. Ovid, & L. Tzeng (Eds.), *In honour of William S.-Y. Wang: Interdisciplinary studies in language and language change* (pp. 187–221). Taiwan: Pyramid.
Doron, E. (1999). Semitic templates as representations of argument structure. In *Proceedings of the TLS Conference on Perspectives on Argument Structure.* University of Texas.
Dowty, D. (1979). *Word meaning and Montague grammar.* Dordrecht: Reidel.
Fodor, J. (1970). Three reasons for not deriving *kill* from *cause to die. Linguistic Inquiry, 1,* 429–438.
Han, P. (2017). A force-theoretic approach to Mandarin single-clause resultative constructions. In *Proceedings of the Annual Conference of the Canadian Linguistic Association* (pp. 1–13).
Harley, H. (2008). On the causative construction. In S. Miyagawa & M. Saito (Eds.), *Handbook of Japanese linguistics* (pp. 20–53). Oxford: Oxford University Press.
Harley, H. (2013). External arguments and the mirror principle: On the distinctness of voice and v. *Lingua, 125,* 34–57.
Her, O. (2007). Argument-function mismatches in Mandarin resultatives: A lexical mapping account. *Lingua, 117,* 221–246.

Huang, C.-T. (2006). Resultatives and unaccusatives: A parametric view. *Bulletin of the Chinese Linguistic Society of Japan, 253,* 1–43.

Kratzer, A. (1996). Severing the external argument from its verb. In J. Rooryck & L. Zaring (Eds.), *Phrase structure and the lexicon* (pp. 109–137). Dordrecht: Kluwer.

Levin, B., & Rappaport Hovav, M. (1995). *Unaccusativity: At the syntax-lexical semantics interface.* Cambridge, MA.: MIT Press.

Li, C. (2008). On the headedness of Mandarin resultative verb compounds. In *Proceedings of the 20th North American Conference on Chinese Linguistics* (NACCL-20) (pp. 735–750). Columbus, Ohio: The Ohio State University.

Li, Y. (1990). On V-V compounds in Chinese. *Natural Language & Linguistic Theory, 8,* 177–207.

Li, Y. (1993). Structural head and aspectuality. *Language, 69,* 480–504.

Li, Y. (1995). The thematic hierarchy and causativity. *Natural Language & Linguistic Theory, 13,* 255–282.

Lin, J. (2004). Event structure and the encoding of arguments: The syntax of the Mandarin and English verb phrase. Doctoral dissertation. Massachusetts Institute of Technology.

Marantz, A. (1991). Case and licensing. In G. Westphal, B. Ao, & H. Chae (Eds.), *Proceedings of Eastern States Conference On Linguistics* (pp. 234–253). Cornell Linguistics Club.

Marantz, A. (2013). Verbal argument structure: Events and participants. *Lingua, 130,* 152–168.

McCawley, J. (1978). Conversational implicature and the lexicon. In P. Cole (Ed.), *Syntax and semantics 9: Pragmatics* (pp. 245–259). New York: Academic Press.

Merchant, J. (2013). Voice and ellipsis. *Linguistic Inquiry, 44,* 77–108.

Neeleman, A., & Van de Koot, J. (2002). The configurational matrix. *Linguistic Inquiry, 33,* 529–574.

Perlmutter, D. (1978). Impersonal passives and the unaccusative hypothesis. In *Proceedings of The Fourth Annual Meeting of the Berkeley Linguistic Society* (pp. 157–189). Berkeley: Berkeley Linguistic Society.

Perlmutter, D., & Postal, P. (1984). The 1-advancement exclusiveness law. In D. Perlmutter & C. Rosen (Eds.), *Studies in relational grammar* (pp. 81–125). Chicago: The University of Chicago Press.

Pylkkänen, L. (2008). *Introducing arguments.* Cambridge, MA: MIT Press.

Rappaport Hovav, M., & Levin, B. (2012). Lexicon uniformity and the causative alternation. In M. Everaert, M. Marelj, & T. Siloni (Eds.), *The theta system: Argument structure at the interface* (pp. 150–176). Oxford, UK: Oxford University Press.

Reinhart, T. (2002). The theta system: An overview. *Theoretical Linguistics, 28,* 229–290.

Schäfer, F. (2008). *The syntax of (Anti-)Causatives: External arguments in change-of-state contexts.* Amsterdam: John Benjamins.

Shibatani, M. (1976). The grammar of causative constructions: A conspectus. In M. Shibatani (Ed.), *Syntax and semantics 6: The grammar of causative constructions* (pp. 1–40). New York: Academic Press.

Vecchiato, A. (2011). Events in the grammar of direct and indirect causation. Doctoral dissertation. University of Southern California.

von Stechow, A. (1996). The different readings of *wieder* 'again': A structural account. *Journal of Semantics, 13,* 87–138.

Wang, C. (2010). The microparametric syntax of resultatives in Chinese languages. Doctoral dissertation. New York University.

Wolff, P. (2003). Direct causation in the linguistic coding and individuation of causal events. *Cognition, 88,* 1–48.

Zhang, N. (2001). The structures of depictive and resultative constructions in Chinese. *ZAS Papers in Linguistics, 22,* 191–221.

Chapter 5
Conclusion and Future Research

5.1 The Present Work: Brief Summary and Its Significance

In this work, I investigated three issues of V-V resultatives in Mandarin within the generative framework: their generation, their syntactic structure, and their alternation properties.

I first considered the generation of two types of V-V compounds, resultative and parallel compounds (Chap. 2). In this work, I first conducted a comparison between these two types of compounds, showing that while they are both composed with two verbs, these two types of V-V compounds demonstrate systematically different properties. Then I demonstrated that the two-domain hypothesis (Marantz, 2000) can provide a coherent explanation for these contrasting properties. I therefore proposed that while parallel V-V compounds are formed in the inner (root) domain, resultative V-V compounds are formed in the outer domain.

This analysis on the generation of resultative and parallel V-V compounds in Mandarin has the following contributions to the field. First, for the first time, this study observed and compared the properties of these two types of V-V compounds in a systematic manner. Secondly, to the best of my knowledge, this is the first time the two-domain hypothesis is applied to analyze data from Mandarin. On the one hand, this hypothesis captures the properties of the Mandarin data in question satisfactorily; on the other hand, data from Mandarin provide empirical support for the two-domain hypothesis.

The second fundamental property of V-V resultatives I explored is their syntactic structures (Chap. 3). I adopted an event-based approach, and compared my analysis with Lin's (2004) influential work. Lin's work demonstrated that this approach not only captures certain properties of these constructions, but also is very promising in analyzing their syntactic structure. On the one hand, the present work is spurred by Lin's work. However, unlike Lin's work, the focus of my analysis is how adverbial modification properties can indicate the syntactic structure of V-V resultatives—to be more specific, which functional heads are present, and how the verb roots are related to these functional heads. Based on adverbial modification properties, my analysis revealed the different structures of object-oriented and subject-oriented V-V resultatives. I argued that object-oriented V-V resultatives are causatives, which contain the two functional heads of v_{CAUSE} and v_{BECOME}, while subject-oriented V-V resultatives are unaccusative predicates, which contain a single v_{BECOME} head.

Compared to Lin's work, this present analysis makes two major contributions. First, it brings the adverbial modification properties of V-V resultatives into the discussion, which leads to observation that the two types V-V resultatives actually have different structures. Second, based on this observation, a causativization vs. decausativization approach to the alternations of certain resultative V-V compounds is proposed, an empirical domain that is not considered in Lin's analysis. Also, comparing to another influential work on V-V resultatives in Mandarin, Li's (2005) work, the present analysis shows that Li's argument that V-V resultative compounds enter syntax as atomic units does not hold.

I then considered two other interrelated properties of V-V resultatives, their subject properties and alternation properties. I demonstrated that while the subject in an object-oriented V-V resultative is an external argument, the subject of a subject-oriented V-V resultative is not. Regarding the alternation properties of V-V resultatives, in previous analyses that assume that all the V-V resultative constructions have the same syntactic structure, there are no categorical differences between the alternations of individual V-V resultatives. Based on my argument that object-oriented and subject-oriented V-V resultatives have different argument structures, I proposed that alternations of V-V resultatives fall into two categories: decausativization of object-oriented V-V resultatives, and causativization of subject-oriented V-V resultatives. I then demonstrated that this categorization, combined with the well-established Direct Causation Condition, can provide a coherent explanation to the complex alternation properties of V-V resultatives.

5.2   Future Studies

In my analysis of the fundamental properties of V-V resultatives in Mandarin, some further interesting questions have been raised. For example, why in generating parallel V-V compounds, it is the abstract meaning of the roots that are employed, while in generating resultative compounds, it is the literal meaning of the roots that are used? This question, unanswered in the present work, deserves further investigation in the future.

This study provided an analysis of the subject-oriented V-V resultatives that carry a surface object. This surface object clearly is not a canonical theme object, and I proposed that it is adjoined to the V_1 root. However, it seems that subject-oriented V-V resultatives carrying a surface object do not all demonstrate the same properties. Particular, in some of them, the surface object does seem to bear a thematic relation to V_2. For this class of V-V resultatives, should the surface object be analyzed as adjoined to the V_2 root? A further and more detailed study on this issue is necessary in the future.

Still another observation of this work is that the alternations of certain resultative V-V compounds seem to demonstrate a higher degree of acceptance when appearing in the *BA*-version of the predicates. The reason for this phenomenon also deserves further exploration in future research.

The present work has focused on just the V-V resultative constructions in Mandarin. Resultative V-V constructions, given that they are composed by two adjacent verbs, can be viewed as a special case of serial verb constructions (SVCs), constructions that are widespread in Mandarin, as well as in other Asian and West African languages. Having gained significant understanding of resultative V-V constructions, the next step of research can be their relation to SVCs, for instance, the similarities and differences between them. This is a complex issue, and future research on this topic will better our understanding of both V-V resultatives and SVCs.

In addition, crosslinguistically, resultative constructions are found in many languages, such as English, and have been a much-studied topic in the literature. To my knowledge, a systematic comparative study of resultative constructions in Mandarin and English has not been done, which can be another significant topic for future study.

However, I will conclude the inquiry here, hoping the questions raised in this study will inspire further studies in the future.

References

Li, Y. (2005). X^0: A theory of the morphology-syntax interface: A theory of the morphology-syntax interface. Cambridge, MA: MIT Press.

Lin, J. (2004). Event structure and the encoding of arguments: The syntax of the Mandarin and English verb phrase. Doctoral dissertation. Massachusetts Institute of Technology.

Marantz, A. (2000). Words. Unpublished ms. Massachusetts Institute of Technology.

Uncited References

Folli, R., & Harley, H. (2012). The syntax of argument structure: Evidence from Italian complex predicates. *Journal of Linguistics, 49*(1), 93–125.

Packard, J. (2000). *The morphology of Chinese: A linguistic and cognitive approach.* Cambridge: Cambridge University Press.

Sproat, R. & Shih, C. (1996). A corpus-based analysis of Mandarin nominal root compound. *Journal of East Asian Linguistics, 5*(1), 49–71. Springer.